LIVING LITURGY™

FOR CANTORS

LIVING LITURGY™

FOR CANTORS

Year A • 2014

Kathleen Harmon, S.N.D. de N.
Joyce Ann Zimmerman, C.PP.S.
Christopher W. Conlon, S.M.

LITURGICAL PRESS
Collegeville, Minnesota

www.litpress.org

Design by Ann Blattner. Art by Martin Erspamer, OSB.

ISSN 1947-2862

ISBN 978-0-8146-3501-8

Presented to

_____

in grateful appreciation
for ministering as a Cantor

_____

_____

(date)

Living Liturgy™ for Cantors is intended to help psalmists prepare themselves to sing the responsorial psalm by reflecting on the text of the psalm in the context of the readings of the day and applying this reflection to a spirituality for daily living. A cantor who has a sense of how the psalm is connected to the readings and to his or her daily living will sing the psalm with greater sensitivity. The cantor's singing will flow out of personal encounter with God who works through the Liturgy of the Word to draw the cantor and the assembly more fully into being who they are: the Body of Christ.

Living Liturgy™ for Cantors contains the gospel readings, first readings, and responsorial psalms for every Sunday of the liturgical year, for those solemnities that are holy days of obligation, and for Ash Wednesday. An appendix contains the second readings for those days (namely, the Sundays of Advent, Christmas, Lent, and Easter; the solemnities; and Ash Wednesday) when that reading has an intended connection to the other readings. For each Sunday or solemnity the book provides a brief reflection on the gospel, a section connecting the psalm to the readings, a suggestion to help the psalmist prepare spiritually to sing the psalm, and a prayer drawn from the readings and the psalm.

While this book is a small one, it offers a wealth of preparatory material for the cantor of the psalm. Cantors might find the following method helpful in using this book, and should feel free to adapt the method or to create another one to suit their needs and situation.

On Monday, read the gospel and spend some time reflecting on its meaning. Ask yourself who Jesus is in this gospel and what he is saying or doing. Who are we, and what are we saying or doing?

On Tuesday, read the first reading. Ask yourself who God is in this reading and what God is saying or doing. Who are we, and what are we saying or doing? Read "Reflecting on Living the Gospel" and see what further insights open up for you.

On Wednesday, look at the text of the psalm and see how it is connected to the readings. During the festal seasons of Advent, Christmas, Lent, and Easter, and for those days that are solemnities, read the second reading.

On Thursday, read "Connecting the Responsorial Psalm to the Readings" and "Psalmist Preparation" and decide how you might implement the suggested spirituality.

On Friday, sing through the psalm, letting your reflection and your daily living add a new dimension to your understanding of the text. Pray the suggested prayer and ask for the grace to do your ministry well.

On Saturday and Sunday, give yourself over to Christ that he may be the voice the assembly hears.

Even more important than musical preparation of the psalm setting is the cantor's prayerful reflection on the meaning of the text and its role in his or her daily living. The cantor who does this kind of preparation discovers that his or her singing is a dialogue with God that mirrors the dialogue going on between God and the assembly in the Liturgy of the Word. A dimension opens up in the cantor's singing that is far deeper than the beauty of his or her voice. What the assembly hears is the cantor's surrender of self to the paschal mystery of Christ, and it is this surrender to which they respond.

Gospel (Matt 24:37-44; L I A)

Jesus said to his disciples: "As it was in the days of Noah, so it will be at the coming of the Son of Man. In those days before the flood, they were eating and drinking, marrying and giving in marriage, up to the day that Noah entered the ark. They did not know until the flood came and carried them all away. So will it be also at the coming of the Son of Man. Two men will be out in the field; one will be taken, and one will be left. Two women will be grinding at the mill; one will be taken, and one will be left. Therefore, stay awake! For you do not know on which day your Lord will come. Be sure of this: if the master of the house had known the hour of night when the thief was coming, he would have stayed awake and not let his house be broken into. So too, you also must be prepared, for at an hour you do not expect, the Son of Man will come."

First Reading (Isa 2:1-5)

This is what Isaiah, son of Amoz, saw concerning Judah and Jerusalem.
In days to come,
the mountain of the LORD's house
shall be established as the highest mountain
and raised above the hills.
All nations shall stream toward it;
many peoples shall come and say:
"Come, let us climb the LORD's mountain,
to the house of the God of Jacob,
that he may instruct us in his ways,
and we may walk in his paths."
For from Zion shall go forth instruction,
and the word of the LORD from Jerusalem.
He shall judge between the nations,
and impose terms on many
peoples.
They shall beat their swords
into plowshares
and their spears into
pruning hooks;
one nation shall not raise the
sword against another,
nor shall they train for war
again.

O house of Jacob, come,
  let us walk in the light of the LORD!

Responsorial Psalm (Ps 122:1-2, 3-4, 4-5, 6-7, 8-9)

℟. Let us go rejoicing to the house of the Lord.

I rejoiced because they said to me,
  "We will go up to the house of the LORD."
And now we have set foot
  within your gates, O Jerusalem.

℟. Let us go rejoicing to the house of the Lord.

Jerusalem, built as a city
  with compact unity.
To it the tribes go up,
  the tribes of the LORD.

℟. Let us go rejoicing to the house of the Lord.

According to the decree for Israel,
  to give thanks to the name of the LORD.
In it are set up judgment seats,
  seats for the house of David.

℟. Let us go rejoicing to the house of the Lord.

Pray for the peace of Jerusalem!
  May those who love you prosper!
May peace be within your walls,
  prosperity in your buildings.

℟. Let us go rejoicing to the house of the Lord.

Because of my brothers and friends
  I will say, "Peace be within you!"
Because of the house of the LORD, our God,
  I will pray for your good.

℟. Let us go rejoicing to the house of the Lord.

See Appendix, p. 210, for Second Reading

Reflecting on Living the Gospel

Humans have been both unfaithful and faithful to God's ways; have not paid attention, have paid attention to God's instructions; have not been awake, have stayed awake to God's comings. The people in the days of Noah did not know that the flood was coming; Jesus' hearers did not know when the Son of Man would come. We, however, do know that Jesus has come, has taught us the way of faithfulness, has brought us salvation. We need only to "stay awake."

Connecting the Responsorial Psalm to the Readings

Isaiah's vision of the future (first reading) sees all nations streaming to God's dwelling place, listening to God's instruction, and living God's ways of peace and justice. Jesus warns us (gospel) to ready ourselves for the coming of the Son of Man when this vision will be fulfilled. Paul (second reading) declares that the hour of fulfillment is now and advises us to act accordingly. Being ready is not a passive state but an active one. We must journey toward the God who is coming toward us. This journey will require twists and turns in our manner of living, but the journey itself will bring us joy (psalm refrain).

Psalmist Preparation

In singing this psalm you express the joy of journeying toward God. This joy has a price, however, for to travel toward God you must leave behind your present dwelling place. In your own life right now where is God calling you to "make a move"? How will making this move prepare you for the final coming of Christ? How in singing this psalm can you encourage the assembly members to make whatever move God is asking of them?

Prayer

God of the future, you call us from our present ways of living to new ways of living in your kingdom. Keep us faithful and alert as we journey toward you in joy. We ask this through Christ our Lord. Amen.

Gospel (Matt 3:1-12; L4A)

John the Baptist appeared, preaching in the desert of Judea and saying, "Repent, for the kingdom of heaven is at hand!" It was of him that the prophet Isaiah had spoken when he said:

> *A voice of one crying out in the desert,*
> *Prepare the way of the LORD,*
> *make straight his paths.*

John wore clothing made of camel's hair and had a leather belt around his waist. His food was locusts and wild honey. At that time Jerusalem, all Judea, and the whole region around the Jordan were going out to him and were being baptized by him in the Jordan River as they acknowledged their sins.

When he saw many of the Pharisees and Sadducees coming to his baptism, he said to them, "You brood of vipers! Who warned you to flee from the coming wrath? Produce good fruit as evidence of your repentance. And do not presume to say to yourselves, 'We have Abraham as our father.' For I tell you, God can raise up children to Abraham from these stones. Even now the ax lies at the root of the trees. Therefore every tree that does not bear good fruit will be cut down and thrown into the fire. I am baptizing you with water, for repentance, but the one who is coming after me is mightier than I. I am not worthy to carry his sandals. He will baptize you with the Holy Spirit and fire. His winnowing fan is in his hand. He will clear his threshing floor and gather his wheat into his barn, but the chaff he will burn with unquenchable fire."

First Reading (Isa 11:1-10)

> On that day, a shoot shall sprout from the stump of Jesse,
>   and from his roots a bud shall blossom.
> The spirit of the LORD shall rest upon him:
>   a spirit of wisdom and of understanding,
> a spirit of counsel and of strength,
>   a spirit of knowledge and of fear of the LORD,
>   and his delight shall be the fear of the LORD.
> Not by appearance shall he judge,
>   nor by hearsay shall he decide,

but he shall judge the poor with justice,
   and decide aright for the land's afflicted.
He shall strike the ruthless with the rod of his mouth,
   and with the breath of his lips he shall slay the wicked.
Justice shall be the band around his waist,
   and faithfulness a belt upon his hips.
Then the wolf shall be a guest of the lamb,
   and the leopard shall lie down with the kid;
the calf and the young lion shall browse together,
   with a little child to guide them.
The cow and the bear shall be neighbors,
   together their young shall rest;
   the lion shall eat hay like the ox.
The baby shall play by the cobra's den,
   and the child lay his hand on the adder's lair.
There shall be no harm or ruin on all my holy mountain;
   for the earth shall be filled with knowledge of the LORD,
   as water covers the sea.
On that day, the root of Jesse,
   set up as a signal for the nations,
the Gentiles shall seek out,
   for his dwelling shall be glorious.

Responsorial Psalm (Ps 72:1-2, 7-8, 12-13, 17)

℟. (cf. 7) Justice shall flourish in his time, and fullness of peace forever.

O God, with your judgment endow the king,
   and with your justice, the king's son;
he shall govern your people with justice
   and your afflicted ones with judgment.

℟. Justice shall flourish in his time, and fullness of peace forever.

Justice shall flower in his days,
   and profound peace, till the moon be no more.
May he rule from sea to sea,
   and from the River to the ends of the earth.

℟. Justice shall flourish in his time, and fullness of peace forever.

For he shall rescue the poor when he cries out,
   and the afflicted when he has no one to help him.

He shall have pity for the lowly and the poor;
the lives of the poor he shall save.

R̂. Justice shall flourish in his time, and fullness of peace forever.

May his name be blessed forever;
as long as the sun his name shall remain.
In him shall all the tribes of the earth be blessed;
all the nations shall proclaim his happiness.

R̂. Justice shall flourish in his time, and fullness of peace forever.

See Appendix, p. 210, for Second Reading

Reflecting on Living the Gospel

John the Baptist prepared "the way of the LORD" by calling the people to repentance so they would not be "thrown into the fire" of "the coming wrath." John announced impending judgment and offered a baptism of repentance. John also announced One to come who would enact that judgment and bring a baptism in the Holy Spirit and fire. The fire of judgment will destroy those who are fruitless; the fire of the Spirit will help the faithful bear good fruit. Advent is, in the end, about jumping into the fire.

Connecting the Responsorial Psalm to the Readings

Psalm 72 was a royal psalm prayed for the king. The Israelites considered the king God's adopted son. His role was to govern in such a way that the nation would remain faithful to covenant living. Because of his governance the poor and the afflicted would be lifted up and the ruthless struck down (first reading, psalm). Christian tradition ascribes Psalm 72 to Christ, the Son sent by God and endowed with divine judgment. Psalm 72 expresses our certainty that the justice and peace we long for will come in Christ. But it also implies that Christ is coming to judge us. The One to come will hold our feet to the fire of his judgment and baptize us with the fire of his righteousness (gospel). As we sing Psalm 72, may we rejoice in the imminence of Christ's coming, and may we also open ourselves to the judgment and justice he will bring.

Psalmist Preparation

The king of whom you sing in this psalm is Christ who will return at the end of time to establish God's kingdom of justice and peace. In what ways do you hasten the coming of this kingdom? How do you bring about peace and justice in your family life? in situations at work? in your parish? in the world community?

Prayer

God of justice, you judge our hearts rightly and call us to repentance. Help our hearts burn with the fire of Christ's righteousness that we may hasten the coming of his kingdom by doing always what is right and just. We ask this through Christ our Lord. Amen.

Gospel (Luke 1:26-38; L689)

The angel Gabriel was sent from God to a town of Galilee called Nazareth, to a virgin betrothed to a man named Joseph, of the house of David, and the virgin's name was Mary. And coming to her, he said, "Hail, full of grace! The Lord is with you." But she was greatly troubled at what was said and pondered what sort of greeting this might be. Then the angel said to her, "Do not be afraid, Mary, for you have found favor with God. Behold, you will conceive in your womb and bear a son, and you shall name him Jesus. He will be great and will be called Son of the Most High, and the Lord God will give him the throne of David his father, and he will rule over the house of Jacob forever, and of his Kingdom there will be no end." But Mary said to the angel, "How can this be, since I have no relations with a man?" And the angel said to her in reply, "The Holy Spirit will come upon you, and the power of the Most High will overshadow you. Therefore the child to be born will be called holy, the Son of God. And behold, Elizabeth, your relative, has also conceived a son in her old age, and this is the sixth month for her who was called barren; for nothing will be impossible for God." Mary said, "Behold, I am the handmaid of the Lord. May it be done to me according to your word." Then the angel departed from her.

First Reading (Gen 3:9-15, 20)

After the man, Adam, had eaten of the tree, the LORD God called to the man and asked him, "Where are you?" He answered, "I heard you in the garden; but I was afraid, because I was naked, so I hid myself." Then he asked, "Who told you that you were naked? You have eaten, then, from the tree of which I had forbidden you to eat!" The man replied, "The woman whom you put here with me— she gave me fruit from the tree, and so I ate it." The LORD God then asked the woman, "Why did you do such a thing?" The woman answered, "The serpent tricked me into it, so I ate it."

Then the LORD God said to the serpent:

"Because you have done this, you shall be banned
    from all the animals
    and from all the wild creatures;

on your belly shall you crawl,
 and dirt shall you eat
 all the days of your life.
I will put enmity between you and the woman,
 and between your offspring and hers;
he will strike at your head,
 while you strike at his heel."

The man called his wife Eve, because she became the mother of all the living.

Responsorial Psalm (Ps 98:1, 2-3, 3-4)

℟. (1a) Sing to the Lord a new song, for he has done marvelous deeds.

Sing to the LORD a new song,
 for he has done wondrous deeds;
his right hand has won victory for him,
 his holy arm.

℟. Sing to the Lord a new song, for he has done marvelous deeds.

The LORD has made his salvation known:
 in the sight of the nations he has revealed his justice.
He has remembered his kindness and his faithfulness
 toward the house of Israel.

℟. Sing to the Lord a new song, for he has done marvelous deeds.

All the ends of the earth have seen
 the salvation by our God.
Sing joyfully to the LORD, all you lands;
 break into song; sing praise.

℟. Sing to the Lord a new song, for he has done marvelous deeds.

See Appendix, p. 210, for Second Reading

Reflecting on Living the Gospel

Mary is twice troubled: first, when the angel Gabriel greets her as one "full of grace" and, second, when she is told she will conceive in spite of having had "no relations with a man." There is also a double gift: first, God's gracious gift to Mary of holiness and the call to bear the incarnate One; second, Mary's gracious gift to us of her yes response, "May it be done to me." The same gifts of God are offered to us, calling forth our own gift of "May it be done to me."

Connecting the Responsorial Psalm to the Readings

Adam and Eve turn away from God in disobedience (first reading). "Why," God anguishes, "did you do such a thing?" God does not respond, however, by turning away from the human family. Instead God works "marvelous deeds" on our behalf (psalm). On this solemnity we celebrate the marvelous deed that God preserved Mary free from all sin in preparation for her role as the new Eve who would bear Christ. We celebrate the marvelous deed that through Christ we have received adoption as God's very own children (second reading). We celebrate the marvelous deed of grace that enabled Mary to say yes to God, reversing the no of the first humans in the garden (gospel). How can we not "Sing to the Lord a new song" (psalm) about the things God does!

Psalmist Preparation

In response to human sin and infidelity God works marvelous deeds of salvation. Where do you see God's saving deeds in your own life? in the life of your family? in the life of the world community? How every day can you sing a new song to the Lord for these marvelous deeds?

Prayer

God of marvelous deeds, you adopt us in Christ as your sons and daughters. May we, like Mary, always say yes to the call of your will and the workings of your grace. We ask this through Christ our Lord. Amen.

Gospel (Matt 11:2-11; L7A)

When John the Baptist heard in prison of the works of the Christ, he sent his disciples to Jesus with this question, "Are you the one who is to come, or should we look for another?" Jesus said to them in reply, "Go and tell

John what you hear and see: the blind regain their sight, the lame walk, lepers are cleansed, the deaf hear, the dead are raised, and the poor have the good news proclaimed to them. And blessed is the one who takes no offense at me."

As they were going off, Jesus began to speak to the crowds about John, "What did you go out to the desert to see? A reed swayed by the wind? Then what did you go out to see? Someone dressed in fine clothing? Those who wear fine clothing are in royal palaces.

Then why did you go out? To see a prophet? Yes, I tell you, and more than a prophet. This is the one about whom it is written:

Behold, I am sending my messenger ahead of you;
he will prepare your way before you.

Amen, I say to you, among those born of women there has been none greater than John the Baptist; yet the least in the kingdom of heaven is greater than he."

First Reading (Isa 35:1-6a, 10)

The desert and the parched land will exult;
     the steppe will rejoice and bloom.
They will bloom with abundant flowers,
     and rejoice with joyful song.
The glory of Lebanon will be given to them,
     the splendor of Carmel and Sharon;
they will see the glory of the LORD,
     the splendor of our God.
Strengthen the hands that are feeble,
     make firm the knees that are weak,
say to those whose hearts are frightened:
     Be strong, fear not!

Here is your God,
   he comes with vindication;
with divine recompense
   he comes to save you.
Then will the eyes of the blind be opened,
   the ears of the deaf be cleared;
then will the lame leap like a stag,
   then the tongue of the mute will sing.

Those whom the LORD has ransomed will return
   and enter Zion singing,
   crowned with everlasting joy;
they will meet with joy and gladness,
   sorrow and mourning will flee.

Responsorial Psalm (Ps 146:6-7, 8-9, 9-10)

R̸. (cf. Isaiah 35:4) Lord, come and save us. *or:* R̸. Alleluia.

The LORD God keeps faith forever,
   secures justice for the oppressed,
   gives food to the hungry.
The LORD sets captives free.

R̸. Lord, come and save us. *or:* R̸. Alleluia.

The LORD gives sight to the blind;
   the LORD raises up those who were bowed down.
The LORD loves the just;
   the LORD protects strangers.

R̸. Lord, come and save us. *or:* R̸. Alleluia.

The fatherless and the widow he sustains,
   but the way of the wicked he thwarts.
The LORD shall reign forever;
   your God, O Zion, through all generations.

R̸. Lord, come and save us. *or:* R̸. Alleluia.

See Appendix, p. 210, for Second Reading

Reflecting on Living the Gospel

The gospel begins with John questioning who Jesus is, and concludes with Jesus extolling who John is. What makes John great is that he recognizes in "the works of the Christ" the person and presence of the Messiah—"the one who is to come." This is exactly our Advent challenge: to see in the goodness around us the works of Jesus and the Presence of "the Christ." Advent calls us to look deeper and then to trust what we see. Whom we discover depends upon what we see.

Connecting the Responsorial Psalm to the Readings

When the Israelites were conquered by Babylon and carried off into exile in 587 BC, the experience threw them into a crisis of faith. Was their God not stronger than pagan gods? Did God not really care about them? Written after Israel's release from Babylon, Psalm 146 reasserts Israel's faith that God can be counted on forever and does indeed care, in a litany of ways, for those in need.

We stand in the same position as Israel. We have the promise of salvation gloriously described in the first reading. We have the witness of the saving works of Jesus detailed in the gospel. Yet we see so much death and destruction, pain and suffering, injustice and evil in the world. In the midst of the reality of the human situation, we need to remain strong (first reading), to "be patient" (second reading), and to examine continually who and what we are looking for (gospel). Psalm 146 tells us what we will see if we keep looking at God.

Psalmist Preparation

About what do you need to remain strong (first reading) and be patient (second reading) as you await the coming of Christ? In what ways does this psalm strengthen your faith in God's promise of salvation?

Prayer

God of tender care, we long for your salvation. Grant us patience and strength as we wait for the coming of your Son, our brother and our savior. We ask this through Christ our Lord. Amen.

Gospel (Matt 1:18-24; L10A)

This is how the birth of Jesus Christ came about. When his mother Mary
was betrothed to Joseph, but before they lived together, she was found
with child through the Holy Spirit. Joseph her husband, since he was a
righteous man, yet unwilling to expose her to shame, decided to divorce
her quietly. Such was his intention when, behold, the angel of the Lord appeared to him in a dream and said, "Joseph, son of David, do not be afraid
to take Mary your wife into your home. For it is through the Holy Spirit
that this child has been conceived
in her. She will bear a son and you
are to name him Jesus, because he
will save his people from their
sins." All this took place to fulfill
what the Lord had said through
the prophet:

> Behold, the virgin shall conceive
> and bear a son,
> and they shall name him
> Emmanuel,

which means "God is with us." When Joseph awoke, he did as the angel
of the Lord had commanded him and took his wife into his home.

First Reading (Isa 7:10-14)

The LORD spoke to Ahaz, saying: Ask for a sign from the LORD, your God;
let it be deep as the netherworld, or high as the sky! But Ahaz answered,
"I will not ask! I will not tempt the LORD!" Then Isaiah said: Listen, O
house of David! Is it not enough for you to weary people, must you also
weary my God? Therefore the Lord himself will give you this sign: the
virgin shall conceive, and bear a son, and shall name him Emmanuel.

Responsorial Psalm (Ps 24:1-2, 3-4, 5-6)

℟. (7c and 10b) Let the Lord enter; he is king of glory.

The LORD's are the earth and its fullness;
  the world and those who dwell in it.
For he founded it upon the seas
  and established it upon the rivers.

℟. Let the Lord enter; he is king of glory.

Who can ascend the mountain of the LORD?
or who may stand in his holy place?
One whose hands are sinless, whose heart is clean,
who desires not what is vain.

R̦. Let the Lord enter; he is king of glory.

He shall receive a blessing from the LORD,
a reward from God his savior.
Such is the race that seeks for him,
that seeks the face of the God of Jacob.

R̦. Let the Lord enter; he is king of glory.

See Appendix, p. 211, for Second Reading

Reflecting on Living the Gospel

In this gospel, the state of affairs is not what it appears to be. Mary is not unfaithful, but faithful. Mary is with child, but a virgin. The infant is not only an earthly child, but also a heavenly One. Yet the infant is not heaven-bound, but an earth-bound Emmanuel. Joseph is not the father, but in a father's role names the Child Jesus. When the Spirit of God is at work, and we cooperate as did Mary and Joseph, something altogether new happens: mystery abounds, "God is with us."

Connecting the Responsorial Psalm to the Readings

Throughout history God manifests salvation through signs that are concrete, specific, and identifiable: swords are beaten into plowshares (see Advent 1); the sinful repent, the unrepentant are punished, and the wolf dines with the lamb (see Advent 2); the blind, deaf, lame are healed (see Advent 3). When Ahaz refuses to ask God for a sign (first reading), he is refusing God entrance into history and into his heart. God can only react with weariness.

Through the unfolding Lectionary readings of this Advent season we have been marking the signs of God's saving work and keeping their tally. We are ready now to stand not with Ahaz but with Joseph who accepted a seemingly impossible sign and did as the Lord commanded (gospel). We are ready now for the most embodied sign of all, the birth of Jesus. We are ready now to shout "Let the Lord enter" (psalm refrain).

Psalmist Preparation

"Let the Lord enter!" On what door into your life is God knocking? Have you done what is needed these past weeks of Advent to clear the way for Christ to enter? What more need you do?

Prayer

Loving God, you come to us in surprising and earthly ways. Open our eyes that we may see your coming and our hearts that we may receive you with joy. We ask this through Christ our Lord. Amen.

Gospel (Matt 1:1-25 [or Matt 1:18-25]; L13ABC)

The book of the genealogy of Jesus Christ, the son of David, the son of Abraham.

Abraham became the father of Isaac, Isaac the father of Jacob, Jacob the father of Judah and his brothers. Judah became the father of Perez and Zerah, whose mother was Tamar. Perez became the father of Hezron, Hezron the father of Ram, Ram the father of Amminadab. Amminadab became the father of Nahshon, Nahshon the father of Salmon, Salmon the father of Boaz, whose mother was Rahab. Boaz became the father of Obed, whose mother was Ruth. Obed became the father of Jesse, Jesse the father of David the king.

David became the father of Solomon, whose mother had been the wife of Uriah. Solomon became the father of Rehoboam, Rehoboam the father of Abijah, Abijah the father of Asaph. Asaph became the father of Jehoshaphat, Jehoshaphat the father of Joram, Joram the father of Uzziah. Uzziah became the father of Jotham, Jotham the father of Ahaz, Ahaz the father of Hezekiah. Hezekiah became the father of Manasseh, Manasseh the father of Amos, Amos the father of Josiah. Josiah became the father of Jechoniah and his brothers at the time of the Babylonian exile.

After the Babylonian exile, Jechoniah became the father of Shealtiel, Shealtiel the father of Zerubbabel, Zerubbabel the father of Abiud. Abiud became the father of Eliakim, Eliakim the father of Azor, Azor the father of Zadok. Zadok became the father of Achim, Achim the father of Eliud, Eliud the father of Eleazar. Eleazar became the father of Matthan, Matthan the father of Jacob, Jacob the father of Joseph, the husband of Mary. Of her was born Jesus who is called the Christ.

Thus the total number of generations from Abraham to David is fourteen generations; from David to the Babylonian exile, fourteen generations; from the Babylonian exile to the Christ, fourteen generations.

Now this is how the birth of Jesus Christ came about. When his mother Mary was betrothed to Joseph, but before they lived together, she was found with child through the Holy Spirit. Joseph her husband, since he was a righteous man, yet unwilling to expose her to shame, decided to divorce her quietly. Such was his intention when, behold, the angel of the Lord appeared to him in a dream and said, "Joseph, son of David, do not be afraid to take Mary your wife into your home. For it is through the Holy Spirit that this child has been conceived in her. She will bear a son and you are to name him Jesus, because he will save his people from their sins." All this took place to fulfill what the Lord had said through the prophet:

> *Behold, the virgin shall conceive and bear a son,*
> *and they shall name him Emmanuel,*

which means "God is with us." When Joseph awoke, he did as the angel of the Lord had commanded him and took his wife into his home. He had no relations with her until she bore a son, and he named him Jesus.

First Reading (Isa 62:1-5)

> For Zion's sake I will not be silent,
>> for Jerusalem's sake I will not be quiet,
> until her vindication shines forth like the dawn
>> and her victory like a burning torch.

> Nations shall behold your vindication,
>> and all the kings your glory;
> you shall be called by a new name
>> pronounced by the mouth of the LORD.
> You shall be a glorious crown in the hand of the LORD,
>> a royal diadem held by your God.
> No more shall people call you "Forsaken,"
>> or your land "Desolate,"
> but you shall be called "My Delight,"
>> and your land "Espoused."
> For the LORD delights in you
>> and makes your land his spouse.
> As a young man marries a virgin,
>> your Builder shall marry you;
> and as a bridegroom rejoices in his bride
>> so shall your God rejoice in you.

Responsorial Psalm (Ps 89:4-5, 16-17, 27, 29)

R̸. (2a) Forever I will sing the goodness of the Lord.

> I have made a covenant with my chosen one,
>> I have sworn to David my servant:
> forever will I confirm your posterity
>> and establish your throne for all generations.

℞. Forever I will sing the goodness of the Lord.

Blessed the people who know the joyful shout;
  in the light of your countenance, O LORD, they walk.
At your name they rejoice all the day,
  and through your justice they are exalted.

℞. Forever I will sing the goodness of the Lord.

He shall say of me, "You are my father,
  my God, the Rock, my savior."
Forever I will maintain my kindness toward him,
  and my covenant with him stands firm.

℞. Forever I will sing the goodness of the Lord.

See Appendix, p. 211, for Second Reading

Reflecting on Living the Gospel
In the beginning of this gospel Joseph is in the dark: he does not know how Mary has become pregnant. When God intervenes through a dream, Joseph sees clearly that he must do "as the angel of the Lord had commanded him." This new light of understanding is the revelation of the mystery of Emmanuel, "God is with us." What a glorious revelation this is! What a glorious light this is!

Connecting the Responsorial Psalm to the Readings
In the first reading for the Christmas Vigil Mass God promises to keep acting until salvation is completed. In the second reading Paul expounds how God has relentlessly acted throughout history for this salvation. With its lengthy genealogy the gospel grounds progress toward salvation in real human history, among real human beings. Although this salvation has been long in coming, its coming has been nonetheless certain thanks to the promise of God given in covenant fidelity (responsorial psalm) and spousal love (first reading). As we anticipate tomorrow the full celebration of the birth of Christ we stand with generations who looked forward to this day. May we with them and with Mary and Joseph perceive in ordinary human events the inbreaking of divine miracle. May we stand with them among the blessed who see and sing of "the goodness of the Lord."

Psalmist Preparation

In this responsorial psalm you sing of the covenant made by God with "my chosen one." Do you recognize yourself as "chosen" by God, as participating in the covenant God made with Israel, David, Mary and Joseph? Do you recognize the assembly as "chosen"? How might this awareness affect your singing of this psalm and your celebration of Christmas?

Prayer

God of salvation, in the fullness of time you sent your Son to be with us in human flesh. May we live always as your children, faithful to your covenant and singing of your goodness. We ask this through Christ our Lord. Amen.

Gospel (Luke 2:1-14; L14ABC)

In those days a decree went out from Caesar Augustus that the whole world should be enrolled. This was the first enrollment, when Quirinius was governor of Syria. So all went to be enrolled, each to his own town. And Joseph too went up from Galilee from the town of Nazareth to Judea, to the city of David that is called Bethlehem, because he was of the house and family of David, to be enrolled with Mary, his betrothed, who was with child. While they were there, the time came for her to have her child,

and she gave birth to her firstborn son. She wrapped him in swaddling clothes and laid him in a manger, because there was no room for them in the inn.

Now there were shepherds in that region living in the fields and keeping the night watch over their flock. The angel of the Lord appeared to them and the glory of the Lord shone around them, and they were struck with great fear. The angel said to them, "Do not be afraid; for behold, I proclaim to you good news of great joy that will be for all the people. For today in the city of David a savior has been born for you who is Christ and Lord. And this will be a sign for you: you will find an infant wrapped in swaddling clothes and lying in a manger." And suddenly there was a multitude of the heavenly host with the angel, praising God and saying:

"Glory to God in the highest
and on earth peace to those on whom his favor rests."

First Reading (Isa 9:1-6)

The people who walked in darkness
have seen a great light;
upon those who dwelt in the land of gloom
a light has shone.
You have brought them abundant joy
and great rejoicing,
as they rejoice before you as at the harvest,
as people make merry when dividing spoils.
For the yoke that burdened them,
the pole on their shoulder,

and the rod of their taskmaster
   you have smashed, as on the day of Midian.
For every boot that tramped in battle,
   every cloak rolled in blood,
   will be burned as fuel for flames.
For a child is born to us, a son is given us;
   upon his shoulder dominion rests.
They name him Wonder-Counselor, God-Hero,
   Father-Forever, Prince of Peace.
His dominion is vast
   and forever peaceful,
from David's throne, and over his kingdom,
   which he confirms and sustains
by judgment and justice,
   both now and forever.
The zeal of the LORD of hosts will do this!

Responsorial Psalm (Ps 96:1-2, 2-3, 11-12, 13)

℟. (Luke 2:11) Today is born our Savior, Christ the Lord.

Sing to the LORD a new song;
   sing to the LORD, all you lands.
Sing to the LORD; bless his name.

℟. Today is born our Savior, Christ the Lord.

Announce his salvation, day after day.
   Tell his glory among the nations;
   among all peoples, his wondrous deeds.

℟. Today is born our Savior, Christ the Lord.

Let the heavens be glad and the earth rejoice;
   let the sea and what fills it resound;
   let the plains be joyful and all that is in them!
Then shall all the trees of the forest exult.

℟. Today is born our Savior, Christ the Lord.

They shall exult before the LORD, for he comes;
   for he comes to rule the earth.
He shall rule the world with justice
   and the peoples with his constancy.

℟. Today is born our Savior, Christ the Lord.

THE NATIVITY OF THE LORD
Mass at Midnight

See Appendix, p. 211, for Second Reading

Reflecting on Living the Gospel
Joseph and Mary must have been beside themselves, arriving at Bethlehem to find "no room for them in the inn." They accept the kind offer of a stable where, in its little light, the great Light of the world is born and the "glory of the Lord" shines forth. Light and glory shine forth in the humble birth of "a savior . . . who is Christ and Lord." May that Light and glory shine forth always!

Connecting the Responsorial Psalm to the Readings
To us human beings who dwell in darkness, burdened and bloodied, the Savior comes (first reading). He comes not in awe and majesty, but born in the night and laid in a manger (gospel). He comes bringing peace, judgment, and justice. He comes to cleanse us so that we are "eager to do what is good" (second reading). The readings for the Mass at Midnight tell us that Christ takes us as we are and enables us to become much more. And so on this most holy night we join the heavens, the seas, even the trees of the forests in rejoicing, for our Savior has been born, and nothing is the same!

Psalmist Preparation
As you prepare to sing this responsorial psalm, use the refrain for daily personal prayer. Let joy and gratitude for the gift of the incarnation fill your heart so that what is in your heart may flow out of your voice when you sing this psalm during the liturgy.

Prayer
God of salvation, you sent your Son to show us light in darkness, hope in hardship, and majesty in littleness. As he took on our humanity, raise us to take on his divinity. We ask this through Christ our Lord. Amen.

DECEMBER 25, 2013

Gospel (Luke 2:15-20; L15ABC)

When the angels went away from them to heaven, the shepherds said to one another, "Let us go, then, to Bethlehem to see this thing that has taken place, which the Lord has made known to us." So they went in haste and found Mary and Joseph, and the infant lying in the manger. When they saw this, they made known the message that had been told them about this child. All who heard it were amazed by what had been told them by the shepherds. And Mary kept all these things, reflecting on them in her heart. Then the shepherds returned, glorifying and praising God for all they had heard and seen, just as it had been told to them.

First Reading (Isa 62:11-12)

See, the LORD proclaims
   to the ends of the earth:
say to daughter Zion,
   your savior comes!
Here is his reward with him,
   his recompense before him.
They shall be called the holy
      people,
   the redeemed of the LORD,
and you shall be called
      "Frequented,"
   a city that is not forsaken.

Responsorial Psalm (Ps 97:1, 6, 11-12)

R̂. A light will shine on us this day: the Lord is born for us.

The LORD is king; let the earth rejoice;
   let the many isles be glad.
The heavens proclaim his justice,
   and all peoples see his glory.

R̂. A light will shine on us this day: the Lord is born for us.

Light dawns for the just;
   and gladness, for the upright of heart.
Be glad in the LORD, you just,
   and give thanks to his holy name.

R̂. A light will shine on us this day: the Lord is born for us.

See Appendix, p. 211, for Second Reading

Reflecting on Living the Gospel
Enlightened by the revelation of the angels, the shepherds go "in haste" to find the Light of the world. Finding this Light "lying in a manger," they hasten to make him known to all whom they meet. Like the shepherds, we too must hear the revelation and hasten to find this same Light of the world. We too must make him known to all whom we meet. The Light shines. Let us be on our way!

Connecting the Responsorial Psalm to the Readings
Psalm 97 is one of a set of songs (Psalms 93, 95–100) celebrating God's kingship over other gods, the forces of nature, and the movements of history. For the cultures of the ancient Near East a god was powerful because of some concrete mighty act. In Psalm 97 God manifests the divine Self in clouds, fire, and lightning, making the earth tremble and mountains melt. While those who worship other gods bend in shame, Israel rejoices and sings God's praises.

The few lines from Psalm 97 chosen for the Mass at Dawn fit the calm and quiet of early morning. The angels singing the midnight theophany of God's glory have dispersed. Now we and the simple shepherds tiptoe to the stable to see what we have been told about, the mighty act of God "lying in a manger" (gospel), "born for us" (psalm refrain) in human flesh.

Psalmist Preparation
What "light" dawns today? For whom? How does your singing this morning participate in this light?

Prayer
God of salvation, today your light dawns upon us in the face of your Son come to us in human flesh. May we, like the simple shepherds, tell about this Child to all the world. We ask this through Christ our Lord. Amen.

Gospel (John 1:1-18 [or John 1:1-5, 9-14]; L16ABC)

In the beginning was the Word,
    and the Word was with God,
    and the Word was God.
He was in the beginning with God.
All things came to be through him,
    and without him nothing came to be.
What came to be through him
        was life,
    and this life was the light of the human
        race;
the light shines in the darkness,
    and the darkness has not overcome it.
A man named John was sent from God. He came
for testimony, to testify to the light, so that all
might believe through him. He was not the light, but came to testify to
the light. The true light, which enlightens everyone, was coming into the
world.

He was in the world,
    and the world came to be through him,
    but the world did not know him.
He came to what was his own,
    but his own people did not accept him.
But to those who did accept him he gave power to become children of
God, to those who believe in his name, who were born not by natural
generation nor by human choice nor by a man's decision but of God.

And the Word became flesh
    and made his dwelling among us,
    and we saw his glory,
    the glory as of the Father's only Son,
    full of grace and truth.
John testified to him and cried out, saying, "This was he of whom I said,
'The one who is coming after me ranks ahead of me because he existed
before me.'" From his fullness we have all received, grace in place of
grace, because while the law was given through Moses, grace and truth
came through Jesus Christ. No one has ever seen God. The only Son, God,
who is at the Father's side, has revealed him.

First Reading (Isa 52:7-10)

How beautiful upon the mountains
    are the feet of him who brings glad tidings,
announcing peace, bearing good news,
    announcing salvation, and saying to Zion,
    "Your God is King!"

Hark! Your sentinels raise a cry,
    together they shout for joy,
for they see directly, before their eyes,
    the LORD restoring Zion.
Break out together in song,
    O ruins of Jerusalem!
For the LORD comforts his people,
    he redeems Jerusalem.
The LORD has bared his holy arm
    in the sight of all the nations;
all the ends of the earth will behold
    the salvation of our God.

Responsorial Psalm (Ps 98:1, 2-3, 3-4, 5-6)

R̸. (3c) All the ends of the earth have seen the saving power of God.

Sing to the LORD a new song,
    for he has done wondrous deeds;
his right hand has won victory for him,
    his holy arm.

R̸. All the ends of the earth have seen the saving power of God.

The LORD has made his salvation known:
    in the sight of the nations he has revealed his justice.
He has remembered his kindness and his faithfulness
    toward the house of Israel.

R̸. All the ends of the earth have seen the saving power of God.

All the ends of the earth have seen
    the salvation by our God.
Sing joyfully to the LORD, all you lands;
    break into song; sing praise.

R̸. All the ends of the earth have seen the saving power of God.

Sing praise to the LORD with the harp,
  with the harp and melodious song.
With trumpets and the sound of the horn
  sing joyfully before the King, the LORD.

R℣. All the ends of the earth have seen the saving power of God.

See Appendix, p. 212, for Second Reading

Reflecting on Living the Gospel

God's Word is an eternal word, present at the beginning of creation and present to us now. God spoke a creative word "In the beginning," incarnated a glorious Word at that first Christmas, and continues to speak to us a saving Word, the "only Son, God." May this Word be for us the "true light" that leads us to the fullness of grace and truth.

Connecting the Responsorial Psalm to the Readings

Psalm 98 is an enthronement psalm celebrating God's sovereignty over all creation and all nations. It uses three typical images—God as king, God as warrior, and God as wielder of power—which can be unsettling if we interpret them only on the literal level of Israel's victory in battle over a political enemy. But when we look deeper into the imagery—and into the core of Israel's faith—we discover a God working tirelessly to transform the order of the world so that the lowly may be uplifted and the righteous blessed. This is a God exercising power to corral the wicked, destroy evil, erase suffering, and end oppression. Such is the good news we bear (first reading). But there is more. The gospel announces that through Christ we share in this transforming power. The whole world can sing about the saving power of God because it sees that power working in and through us.

Psalmist Preparation

You call the assembly not only to sing about the saving power of God revealed in the birth of Jesus but to show that power to the world by the manner in which they live. How might you grow in your own confidence in this power of God within you?

Prayer

God of salvation, you sent your Word Jesus to dwell among us so that through him we might become your children. Lead us always to live as your daughters and sons who speak only your Word and spread only your Light. We ask this through Christ our Lord. Amen.

Gospel (Matt 2:13-15, 19-23; L17A)

When the magi had departed, behold, the angel of the Lord appeared to Joseph in a dream and said, "Rise, take the child and his mother, flee to Egypt, and stay there until I tell you. Herod is going to search for the child to destroy him." Joseph rose and took the child and his mother by night and departed for Egypt. He stayed there until the death of Herod, that what the Lord had said through the prophet might be fulfilled,

Out of Egypt I called my son.

When Herod had died, behold, the angel of the Lord appeared in a dream to Joseph in Egypt and said, "Rise, take the child and his mother and go to the land of Israel, for those who sought the child's life are dead." He rose, took the child and his mother, and went to the land of Israel. But when he heard that Archelaus was ruling over Judea in place of his father Herod, he was afraid to go back there. And because he had been warned in a dream, he departed for the region of Galilee. He went and dwelt in a town called Nazareth, so that what had been spoken through the prophets might be fulfilled,

He shall be called a Nazorean.

First Reading (Sir 3:2-6, 12-14)

God sets a father in honor over his children;
   a mother's authority he confirms over her sons.
Whoever honors his father atones for sins,
   and preserves himself from them.
When he prays, he is heard;
   he stores up riches who reveres his mother.
Whoever honors his father is gladdened by children,
   and, when he prays, is heard.
Whoever reveres his father will live a long life;
   he who obeys his father brings comfort to his mother.

My son, take care of your father when he is old;
   grieve him not as long as he lives.

Even if his mind fail, be considerate of him;
    revile him not all the days of his life;
kindness to a father will not be forgotten,
    firmly planted against the debt of your sins
    —a house raised in justice to you.

Responsorial Psalm (Ps 128:1-2, 3, 4-5)

℟. (cf. 1) Blessed are those who fear the Lord and walk in his ways.

Blessed is everyone who fears the LORD,
    who walks in his ways!
For you shall eat the fruit of your handiwork;
    blessed shall you be, and favored.

℟. Blessed are those who fear the Lord and walk in his ways.

Your wife shall be like a fruitful vine
    in the recesses of your home;
your children like olive plants
    around your table.

℟. Blessed are those who fear the Lord and walk in his ways.

Behold, thus is the man blessed
    who fears the LORD.
The LORD bless you from Zion:
    may you see the prosperity of Jerusalem
    all the days of your life.

℟. Blessed are those who fear the Lord and walk in his ways.

See Appendix, p. 212, for Second Reading

Reflecting on Living the Gospel

All the wonderful gifts of grace bestowed upon the Holy Family—Jesus' miraculous conception by the Holy Spirit, the virgin birth—did not preserve this family from hardship. They faced challenges and pressures. Yet they responded faithfully and obediently to God's messages and will for them. The Holy Family was not exempt from life-threatening difficulties. Rather, it was in the midst of difficulty that their holiness was tested, deepened, and revealed as a faithful and obedient response to God. This feast calls us to be this same kind of holy family.

THE HOLY FAMILY OF JESUS, MARY, AND JOSEPH

Connecting the Responsorial Psalm to the Readings

The patriarchal context of Psalm 128 can be off-putting to us who live in modern Western culture. But we must look beneath its patriarchal imagery to its promise of blessedness for all people who live according to the way of God. Living God's way means reverencing our parents throughout all the stages of their lives (first reading). It means bearing compassion and patience toward one another, offering forgiveness to those who have hurt us, and remaining faithful to the word of Christ (second reading). It means discerning the will of God for our lives, no matter the form of its deliverance or the level of self-sacrifice demanded (gospel). As Psalm 128 indicates, choosing to live in such a way will bear fruit not only for ourselves and our immediate family but for all the people of God.

Psalmist Preparation

In this responsorial psalm you sing about families related by blood and the family of the church related by baptism. How does your fidelity to God help you in your family relationships? How does it shape your relationship with the church?

Prayer

God, you are a Trinity of Persons who have created us to live in loving relationship with one another. Keep us faithful to our covenant relationship with you and with each other that we may be blessed and favored in your sight. We ask this through Christ our Lord. Amen.

Gospel (Luke 2:16-21; L18ABC)

The shepherds went in haste to Bethlehem and found Mary and Joseph, and the infant lying in the manger. When they saw this, they made known the message that had been told them about this child. All who heard it were amazed by what had been told them by the shepherds. And Mary kept all these

things, reflecting on them in her heart. Then the shepherds returned, glorifying and praising God for all they had heard and seen, just as it had been told to them.

When eight days were completed for his circumcision, he was named Jesus, the name given him by the angel before he was conceived in the womb.

First Reading (Num 6:22-27)

The LORD said to Moses: "Speak to Aaron and his sons and tell them: This is how you shall bless the Israelites. Say to them:

> The LORD bless you and keep you!
> The LORD let his face shine upon you, and be gracious to you!
> The LORD look upon you kindly and give you peace!

So shall they invoke my name upon the Israelites, and I will bless them."

Responsorial Psalm (Ps 67:2-3, 5, 6, 8)

℟. (2a) May God bless us in his mercy.

May God have pity on us and bless us;
    may he let his face shine upon us.
So may your way be known upon earth;
    among all nations, your salvation.

℟. May God bless us in his mercy.

May the nations be glad and exult
    because you rule the peoples in equity;
    the nations on the earth you guide.

℟. May God bless us in his mercy.

May the peoples praise you, O God;
  may all the peoples praise you!
May God bless us,
  and may all the ends of the earth fear him!
R̖. May God bless us in his mercy.

See Appendix, p. 212, for Second Reading

Reflecting on Living the Gospel
Mary opened her entire being to God, contemplating the Word in her heart and bearing the Word in her body. We most fully imitate our mother Mary when we ourselves contemplate God's Word in our hearts and embody that Word in our daily living. What characterizes Mary, then, and all of us who call her mother is openness to God's Presence, contemplation of that divine Presence and what it means for our daily living, and obedience to God's will for us.

Connecting the Responsorial Psalm to the Readings
The Lectionary omits the verse from Psalm 67 which marks it as a song of thanksgiving for a bountiful harvest: "The earth has yielded its harvest; God, our God, blesses us" (v. 7, NABRE). In singing Psalm 67 the Israelites not only thanked God for all that had been given to them but also asked God to extend this bounty to all peoples. On this solemnity we celebrate that the mercy of God has caused the earthly flesh of Mary to yield its greatest blessing, the body of Jesus (gospel). And through this blessing we are harvested as God's own children (second reading). In singing Psalm 67 we acknowledge the unimaginable magnitude of God's mercy toward us, and we pray that all peoples come to know their blessedness in Christ.

Psalmist Preparation
As you prepare to sing Psalm 67, reflect on how blessed you are because of the birth of Christ. Do you know that you are a child of God? Do you know how favored you are? What might you do this week to lead others to discover their blessedness?

Prayer
Saving God, you brought the mystery of salvation to fulfillment in the flesh of Mary. May we, with her, contemplate this wondrous blessing that brings heaven to earth. We ask this through Christ our Lord. Amen.

Gospel (Matt 2:1-12; L20ABC)

When Jesus was born in Bethlehem of Judea, in the days of King Herod, behold, magi from the east arrived in Jerusalem, saying, "Where is the newborn king of the Jews? We saw his star at its rising and have come to do him homage." When King Herod heard this, he was greatly troubled, and all Jerusalem with him. Assembling all the chief priests and the scribes of the people, he inquired of them where the Christ was to be born. They said to him, "In Bethlehem of Judea, for thus it has been written through the prophet:

> *And you, Bethlehem, land of Judah,*
> *   are by no means least among the rulers of Judah;*
> *since from you shall come a ruler,*
> *   who is to shepherd my people Israel."*

Then Herod called the magi secretly and ascertained from them the time of the star's appearance. He sent them to Bethlehem and said, "Go and search diligently for the child. When you have found him, bring me word, that I too may go and do him homage." After their audience with the king they set out. And behold, the star that they had seen at its rising preceded them, until it came and stopped over the place where the child was. They were overjoyed at seeing the star, and on entering the house they saw the child with Mary his mother. They prostrated themselves and did him homage. Then they opened their treasures and offered him gifts of gold, frankincense, and myrrh. And having been warned in a dream not to return to Herod, they departed for their country by another way.

First Reading (Isa 60:1-6)

Rise up in splendor, Jerusalem!
Your light has come,
    the glory of the Lord shines
        upon you.
See, darkness covers the earth,
    and thick clouds cover the
        peoples;
but upon you the LORD shines,
    and over you appears his glory.
Nations shall walk by your light,
    and kings by your shining radiance.

Raise your eyes and look about;
they all gather and come to you:
your sons come from afar,
and your daughters in the arms of their nurses.

Then you shall be radiant at what you see,
your heart shall throb and overflow,
for the riches of the sea shall be emptied out before you,
the wealth of nations shall be brought to you.
Caravans of camels shall fill you,
dromedaries from Midian and Ephah;
all from Sheba shall come
bearing gold and frankincense,
and proclaiming the praises of the LORD.

Responsorial Psalm (Ps 72:1-2, 7-8, 10-11, 12-13)

℟. (cf. 11) Lord, every nation on earth will adore you.

O God, with your judgment endow the king,
and with your justice, the king's son;
he shall govern your people with justice
and your afflicted ones with judgment.

℟. Lord, every nation on earth will adore you.

Justice shall flower in his days,
and profound peace, till the moon be no more.
May he rule from sea to sea,
and from the River to the ends of the earth.

℟. Lord, every nation on earth will adore you.

The kings of Tarshish and the Isles shall offer gifts;
the kings of Arabia and Seba shall bring tribute.
All kings shall pay him homage,
all nations shall serve him.

℟. Lord, every nation on earth will adore you.

For he shall rescue the poor when he cries out,
and the afflicted when he has no one to help him.
He shall have pity for the lowly and the poor;
the lives of the poor he shall save.

℟. Lord, every nation on earth will adore you.

See Appendix, p. 213, for Second Reading

Reflecting on Living the Gospel

Arriving at Jerusalem, the magi thought they had come to the birthplace of "the newborn king of the Jews." The "newborn king," however, was in Bethlehem, the home of David before he was made king, when he was still a simple shepherd boy. This king "who is to shepherd . . . Israel" was not born in a palace, but in a humble abode; was not given homage by Jewish elite, but by foreigners; was not given only gifts acknowledging his kingship, but also a gift of myrrh pointing to his passion. This is no ordinary king being manifested to the world!

Connecting the Responsorial Psalm to the Readings

In Psalm 72 the Israelites prayed for their king. At the time of Christ, however, no king had governed Israel for nearly six hundred years (Herod was merely a figurehead, Rome the real ruler). Psalm 72, if prayed at all then, would have been a petition for the coming of the new king, the Messiah. The early church quickly adopted this psalm as a prefiguring of Christ.

We can readily see the connections between the psalm and the first reading and gospel. Psalm 72 is our prayer that the reign of God in Christ will come about, that leaders of nations will lay their power and wealth at the service of God's redemptive plan, and that justice for the poor and afflicted will be secured. As we sing this psalm, then, we pray that the future which broke into the world with the birth of Christ those many centuries ago may come to be in the present.

Psalmist Preparation

In what ways do you search for the kingdom of Christ? How—in your family relationships, in your job situation, in your neighborhood, for example—do you work for the coming of his kingdom?

Prayer

God of salvation, you sent your Son to be Light in the world's darkness. Fill us with his goodness and grace that we may radiate your glory to all whom we meet. We ask this through Christ our Lord. Amen.

***Gospel* (Matt 3:13-17; L21A)**

Jesus came from Galilee to John at the Jordan to be baptized by him. John tried to prevent him, saying, "I need to be baptized by you, and yet you are coming to me?" Jesus said to him in reply, "Allow it now, for thus it is fitting for us to fulfill all righteousness." Then he allowed him. After Jesus was baptized, he came up from the water and behold, the heavens were opened for him, and he saw the Spirit of God descending like a dove and coming upon him. And a voice came from the heavens, saying, "This is my beloved Son, with whom I am well pleased."

***First Reading* (Isa 42:1-4, 6-7)**

Thus says the LORD:
　　Here is my servant whom I uphold,
　　　　my chosen one with whom I am pleased,
　　upon whom I have put my spirit;
　　　　he shall bring forth justice to the nations,
　　not crying out, not shouting,
　　　　not making his voice heard in the street.
　　A bruised reed he shall not break,
　　　　and a smoldering wick he shall not quench,
　　until he establishes justice on the earth;
　　　　the coastlands will wait for his teaching.

　　I, the LORD, have called you for the victory of justice,
　　　　I have grasped you by the hand;
　　I formed you, and set you
　　　　as a covenant of the people,
　　　　a light for the nations,
　　to open the eyes of the blind,
　　　　to bring out prisoners from confinement,
　　　　and from the dungeon, those who live in darkness.

Responsorial Psalm (Ps 29:1-2, 3-4, 9-10)

R̸. (11b) The Lord will bless his people with peace.

Give to the LORD, you sons of God,
    give to the LORD glory and praise,
give to the LORD the glory due his name;
    adore the LORD in holy attire.

R̸. The Lord will bless his people with peace.

The voice of the LORD is over the waters,
    the LORD, over vast waters.
The voice of the LORD is mighty;
    the voice of the LORD is majestic.

R̸. The Lord will bless his people with peace.

The God of glory thunders,
    and in his temple all say, "Glory!"
The LORD is enthroned above the flood;
    the LORD is enthroned as king forever.

R̸. The Lord will bless his people with peace.

See Appendix, p. 213, for Second Reading

Reflecting on Living the Gospel

Jesus comes to John who is baptizing in the River Jordan. John is pointing to a baptism greater than his and to a person greater than him. Jesus
asks John to baptize him in order to "fulfill all righteousness" and thus
show forth his continuity with the tradition in which John stands. But
more happens. When the heavens open, the Spirit descends, and Jesus is
announced as the "beloved Son," a new tradition is born, and humanity's
relationship with God is changed forever. Through baptism we are invited into this new tradition.

Connecting the Responsorial Psalm to the Readings

In Psalm 29, God's voice is mighty, majestic, and thunderous. In verses
not used in the Lectionary, God's voice shatters cedars, splits oak trees,
strips forests, and rocks the wilderness. To this divine thundering the
people shout back, "Glory!" Today's readings are not full of shouts and
shatterings, however, but of a quiet presence which protects and heals
(first reading), of a divine word of peace (second reading), and of an

intimate proclamation of sonship (gospel). So why all the shouting in the responsorial psalm? Because the One who leads the shouting undergirds the people with strength, blesses them with peace, and leads them to freedom. Because the voice of God wears human flesh, speaks human words, and submits to human customs (gospel). Because the mission of Christ shatters the kingdom of darkness. The psalm reminds us—and the powers of evil—not to be misled by the gentleness of God's entry in Christ.

Psalmist Preparation
Psalm 29 depicts God's ultimate power over the forces of nature. For the Israelites this power revealed God's sovereignty over all the forces of history, seen and unseen. It is this power which becomes present in the baptism and mission of Jesus (gospel). Where do you see this power revealed in today's world? When do you experience yourself sharing in this power?

Prayer
Omnipotent God, in the waters of baptism you flood us with your grace and goodness. Help us take up our baptismal mission to be this grace and goodness in the world. We ask this through Christ our Lord. Amen.

JANUARY 19, 2014

Gospel (John 1:29-34; L64A)

John the Baptist saw Jesus coming toward him and said, "Behold, the Lamb of God, who takes away the sin of the world. He is the one of whom I said, 'A man is coming after me who ranks ahead of me because he existed before me.' I did not know him, but the reason why I came baptizing with water was that he might be made known to Israel." John testified further, saying, "I saw the Spirit come down like a dove from heaven and remain upon him. I did not know him, but the one who sent me to baptize with water told me, 'On whomever you see the Spirit come down and remain, he is the one who will baptize with the Holy Spirit.' Now I have seen and testified that he is the Son of God."

First Reading (Isa 49:3, 5-6)

The LORD said to me: You are my
    servant,
    Israel, through whom I show my
        glory.
Now the LORD has spoken
    who formed me as his servant
        from the womb,
that Jacob may be brought back to
    him

    and Israel gathered to him;
    and I am made glorious in the sight
        of the LORD,
        and my God is now my strength!
It is too little, the LORD says, for you to be my servant,
    to raise up the tribes of Jacob,
    and restore the survivors of Israel;
I will make you a light to the nations,
    that my salvation may reach to the ends of the earth.

Responsorial Psalm (Ps 40:2, 4, 7-8, 8-9, 10)

℟. (8a and 9a) Here am I, Lord; I come to do your will.

I have waited, waited for the LORD,
    and he stooped toward me and heard my cry.
And he put a new song into my mouth,
    a hymn to our God.

℟. Here am I, Lord; I come to do your will.

Sacrifice or offering you wished not,
    but ears open to obedience you gave me.
Holocausts or sin-offerings you sought not;
    then said I, "Behold I come."

℟. Here am I, Lord; I come to do your will.

"In the written scroll it is prescribed for me,
    to do your will, O my God, is my delight,
and your law is within my heart!"

℟. Here am I, Lord; I come to do your will.

I announced your justice in the vast assembly;
    I did not restrain my lips, as you, O LORD, know.

℟. Here am I, Lord; I come to do your will.

Second Reading (1 Cor 1:1-3)

Reflecting on Living the Gospel

This gospel is a testimony of what John has come to know about who
Jesus is: Lamb of God, One who forgives sins, One who preexists, One
who is Spirit-filled, One who baptizes with the Holy Spirit, Son of God.
But John's testimony does not exhaust the richness of Jesus' identity;
there is even more. The mystery of who Jesus is continues to be revealed
to us and through us today. What more are we discovering? What more
are we revealing?

Connecting the Responsorial Psalm to the Readings

In the first strophe of this responsorial psalm we "wait" for the Lord. We
keep watch, and we expect. In the final strophe we "announce" that we
have found the Lord. We testify, we proclaim. Like John the Baptist part
of our mission as disciples is to keep on the lookout for the appearance
of Christ, and then testify to his presence when he does appear. And this
is the obedience we sing about in the middle strophes of the psalm.

As we begin once more our discipleship journey through Ordinary
Time we offer ourselves to God as obedient servants (first reading,
psalm). We set out to find Jesus in every aspect of life. We begin "not
knowing" entirely where and how he will appear (gospel). We end meeting him face to face, and showing others who he is.

Psalmist Preparation

What does it mean to do God's will? In the context of this Sunday's readings it means to search for Christ and then announce his presence to others. As part of your preparation this week choose a specific place to search for Christ, i.e., within your family, in a situation at work, with someone who is suffering, etc., so that the assembly can hear in your voice the testimony of a heart speaking from experience.

Prayer

God of salvation, you sent your Son Jesus to fulfill your covenant with your people. Help us to know him better so that, like him, we may give you our hearts in obedient service. We ask this through Christ our Lord. Amen.

Gospel (Matt 4:12-23 [or Matt 4:12-17]; L67A)

When Jesus heard that John had been arrested, he withdrew to Galilee.
He left Nazareth and went to live in Capernaum by the sea, in the region
of Zebulun and Naphtali, that what had been said through Isaiah the
prophet might be fulfilled:

> Land of Zebulun and land of Naphtali,
>   the way to the sea, beyond the Jordan,
>   Galilee of the Gentiles,
> the people who sit in darkness have seen a great light,
> on those dwelling in a land overshadowed by death
>   light has arisen.

From that time on, Jesus began to
preach and say, "Repent, for the kingdom of heaven is at hand."

As he was walking by the Sea of Galilee, he saw two brothers, Simon who is
called Peter, and his brother Andrew,
casting a net into the sea; they were fishermen. He said to them, "Come after me,
and I will make you fishers of men." At
once they left their nets and followed
him. He walked along from there and
saw two other brothers, James, the son
of Zebedee, and his brother John. They were in a boat, with their father
Zebedee, mending their nets. He called them, and immediately they left
their boat and their father and followed him. He went around all of Galilee, teaching in their synagogues, proclaiming the gospel of the kingdom,
and curing every disease and illness among the people.

First Reading (Isa 8:23–9:3)

First the Lord degraded the land of Zebulun and the land of Naphtali;
but in the end he has glorified the seaward road, the land west of the Jordan, the District of the Gentiles.

> Anguish has taken wing, dispelled is darkness:
>   for there is no gloom where but now there was distress.

> The people who walked in darkness
>   have seen a great light;
>   upon those who dwelt in the land of gloom a light has shone.

You have brought them abundant joy
  and great rejoicing,
as they rejoice before you as at the harvest,
  as people make merry when dividing spoils.
For the yoke that burdened them,
  the pole on their shoulder,
and the rod of their taskmaster
  you have smashed, as on the day of Midian.

Responsorial Psalm **(Ps 27:1, 4, 13-14)**

℟. (1a) The Lord is my light and my salvation.

The LORD is my light and my salvation;
  whom should I fear?
The LORD is my life's refuge;
  of whom should I be afraid?

℟. The Lord is my light and my salvation.

One thing I ask of the LORD;
  this I seek:
to dwell in the house of the LORD
  all the days of my life,
that I may gaze on the loveliness of the LORD
  and contemplate his temple.

℟. The Lord is my light and my salvation.

I believe that I shall see the bounty of the LORD
  in the land of the living.
Wait for the LORD with courage;
  be stouthearted, and wait for the LORD.

℟. The Lord is my light and my salvation.

Second Reading **(1 Cor 1:10-13, 17)**

Reflecting on Living the Gospel
With his arrest, John the Baptist's ministry is finished and Jesus inaugu-
rates a new reality. In him humanity moves from darkness into "a great
light." In him new teaching happens. In him new healing comes. In him
new Life is given. To bring this new reality to completion, Jesus calls Peter
and Andrew, James and John to leave their life as they knew it, to step into
the light and become disciples who proclaim the "gospel of the kingdom."

Connecting the Responsorial Psalm to the Readings

In the first reading God has acted: the people who dwelt in darkness (i.e., death, destruction, despair) now dwell in light (i.e., life, prosperity, hope). The responsorial psalm sings about God's luminous and saving presence. The psalmist asks to dwell always in this presence in order to contemplate the beauty of God and to lead others to "stouthearted" hope in salvation.

The psalmist asks to dwell with God, but in the gospel Jesus invites the apostles to "come" and be with him. Jesus invites them to see him as the luminous and saving presence of God. We, too, are invited to acknowledge Jesus as "light" and "salvation" (psalm). We, too, are invited to dwell within the circle of Jesus' presence and to participate in his mission. This will require a change in our way of living but it will bring the hope of salvation to all the world.

Psalmist Preparation

The responsorial psalm invites you to see in Jesus the full light of God's presence on earth and the coming of salvation to all peoples. Your singing of these verses must arise from your own real desire to see God and to know salvation. When are you most aware of experiencing this desire? What supports this desire in you? What impedes it?

Prayer

Lord of light and salvation, we long to see your dwelling place. Keep us fearless and stouthearted as we await the fullness of the redemption you have promised us. We ask this through Christ our Lord. Amen.

Gospel (Luke 2:22-32 [or 2:22-40]; L524)

When the days were completed for their
    purification
according to the law of Moses,
Mary and Joseph took Jesus up to
    Jerusalem
to present him to the Lord,
just as it is written in the law of the Lord,
*Every male that opens the womb shall be
    consecrated to the Lord,*
and to offer the sacrifice of
a pair of turtledoves or two young pigeons,
in accordance with the dictate in the law of the Lord.

Now there was a man in Jerusalem whose name was Simeon.
This man was righteous and devout,
    awaiting the consolation of Israel,
    and the Holy Spirit was upon him.
It had been revealed to him by the Holy Spirit
    that he should not see death
    before he had seen the Christ of the Lord.
He came in the Spirit into the temple;
    and when the parents brought in the child Jesus
    to perform the custom of the law in regard to him,
    he took him into his arms and blessed God, saying:
        "Now, Master, you may let your servant go
            in peace, according to your word,
        for my eyes have seen your salvation,
            which you prepared in sight of all the peoples,
        a light for revelation to the Gentiles,
        and glory for your people Israel."

First Reading (Mal 3:1-4)

    Thus says the Lord God:
Lo, I am sending my messenger
    to prepare the way before me;
and suddenly there will come to the temple
    the Lord whom you seek,
and the messenger of the covenant whom you desire.

Yes, he is coming, says the LORD of hosts.
But who will endure the day of his coming?
    And who can stand when he appears?
For he is like the refiner's fire,
    or like the fuller's lye.
He will sit refining and purifying silver,
    and he will purify the sons of Levi,
refining them like gold or like silver
    that they may offer due sacrifice to the LORD.
Then the sacrifice of Judah and Jerusalem
    will please the LORD,
    as in the days of old, as in years gone by.

Responsorial Psalm (Ps 24:7, 8, 9, 10)

R̸. (8) Who is this king of glory? It is the Lord!

Lift up, O gates, your lintels;
    reach up, you ancient portals,
    that the king of glory may come in!

R̸. Who is this king of glory? It is the Lord!

Who is this king of glory?
    The LORD, strong and mighty,
    the LORD, mighty in battle.

R̸. Who is this king of glory? It is the Lord!

Lift up, O gates, your lintels;
    reach up, you ancient portals,
    that the king of glory may come in!

R̸. Who is this king of glory? It is the Lord!

Who is this king of glory?
    The LORD of hosts; he is the king of glory.

R̸. Who is this king of glory? It is the Lord!

See Appendix, p. 213, for Second Reading

Reflecting on Living the Gospel
Simeon and Anna show us that more is necessary than obedience to the
law in order to recognize the presence of the Son-Messiah. Filled with expectation, they were actively waiting and looking for "the Christ of the

Lord" and the "redemption of Jerusalem." Their very expectation and waiting was the work of the Holy Spirit within them. As with Simeon and Anna, our own lives must be filled with the expectation and waiting that is truly the work of the Holy Spirit within us. Only then will we see and recognize the Messiah in our midst.

Connecting the Responsorial Psalm to the Readings

The Israelites sang Psalm 24 as part of a ceremony in which they carried the ark into the temple and recommitted themselves to their covenant relationship with God. The psalm declares that all the earth belongs to God who made it, that only the clean of heart may ascend the mountain of God, and orders the temple doorways to open themselves to let God enter.

On the feast of the Presentation the Lectionary uses only the verses related to God's entrance into the temple. In singing these verses, we celebrate the Messiah's entrance into the temple in the person of the infant Jesus. With all the earth and all nations we cry out, "Lift up, O gates . . . that the king of glory may come in!" With Simeon and Anna we acknowledge the fulfillment of what our faithful living, prayer, and expectation continually await: the revelation of salvation present in our midst.

Psalmist Preparation

The portals you open as you sing this responsorial psalm are your eyes that you may recognize Christ, the Savior, present among us. The gates you lift are the doorway to your heart that Christ may take up residence there. You announce that you have recognized who "the king of glory" is, have made him the center of your life, and wish all who hear you to do the same. Who has helped you recognize Christ as the Messiah? Who has helped you see where Christ is present?

Prayer

God of glory, you sent the Son for our salvation. Send us your Spirit that we may recognize the presence of the Savior in our midst, open our hearts to receive him, and live in such a way that he becomes visible to all the world. We ask this through Christ our Lord. Amen.

Gospel (Matt 5:13-16; L73A)

Jesus said to his disciples: "You are the salt of the earth. But if salt loses its taste, with what can it be seasoned? It is no longer good for anything but to be thrown out and trampled underfoot. You are the light of the world. A city set on a mountain cannot be hidden. Nor do they light a lamp and then put it under a bushel basket; it is set on a lampstand, where it gives light to all in the house.

Just so, your light must shine before others, that they may see your good deeds and glorify your heavenly Father."

First Reading (Isa 58:7-10)

Thus says the LORD:
Share your bread with the hungry,
  shelter the oppressed and the homeless;
clothe the naked when you see them,
  and do not turn your back on your own.
Then your light shall break forth like the dawn,
  and your wound shall quickly be healed;
your vindication shall go before you,
  and the glory of the LORD shall be your rear guard.
Then you shall call, and the LORD will answer,
  you shall cry for help, and he will say: Here I am!
If you remove from your midst
  oppression, false accusation and malicious speech;
if you bestow your bread on the hungry
  and satisfy the afflicted;
then light shall rise for you in the darkness,
  and the gloom shall become for you like midday.

Responsorial Psalm (Ps 112:4-5, 6-7, 8-9)

℟. (4a) The just man is a light in darkness to the upright. *or:* ℟. Alleluia.

Light shines through the darkness for the upright;
  he is gracious and merciful and just.

Well for the man who is gracious and lends,
who conducts his affairs with justice.
℟. The just man is a light in darkness to the upright. *or:* ℟. Alleluia.

He shall never be moved;
the just one shall be in everlasting remembrance.
An evil report he shall not fear;
his heart is firm, trusting in the LORD.
℟. The just man is a light in darkness to the upright. *or:* ℟. Alleluia.

His heart is steadfast; he shall not fear.
Lavishly he gives to the poor;
his justice shall endure forever;
his horn shall be exalted in glory.
℟. The just man is a light in darkness to the upright. *or:* ℟. Alleluia.

Second Reading (1 Cor 2:1-5)

Reflecting on Living the Gospel
Jesus uses the metaphors of salt and light to describe the mission of the
disciples. Both metaphors carry positive and negative import. Salt en-
hances, but is thrown away and trampled if it becomes tasteless. Light
shines, but is ineffective if it is hidden. Jesus is clearly saying that disciples must spend themselves in preserving and carrying forward his
saving mission. Disciples must season the world with God's word and
faithfully shine forth God's Presence. The choice is ours: to season or be
discarded, to shine or be hidden.

Connecting the Responsorial Psalm to the Readings
In this Sunday's gospel Jesus commands us to let our light shine so that
others may see our good deeds and offer God praise. The first reading
and psalm indicate the good deeds we are to do: we are to feed the hungry, shelter the homeless, clothe the naked, free the oppressed, and give
to the poor. We are, in other words, to set right what is wrong in the
world. Such deeds of justice will make us "a light in darkness" (psalm refrain), God's own glory will surround us (first reading), and what we
have done will remain forever (psalm).

Psalmist Preparation

Who has taught you what it means to live as a just person? Who do you see shedding light into the darkness of the world? How do you live and act as they do?

Prayer

God of all goodness, you call us to be the salt of your justice and the light of your compassion in the world. Help us to lead all we meet to taste and see how good you are. We ask this through Christ our Lord. Amen.

Gospel (Matt 5:17-37 [or shorter form below Matt 5:20-22a, 27-28, 33-34a, 37]; L76A)

Jesus said to his disciples: "I tell you, unless your righteousness surpasses that of the scribes and Pharisees, you will not enter the kingdom of heaven.

"You have heard that it was said to your ancestors,

You shall not kill; and whoever kills will be liable to judgment.

But I say to you, whoever is angry with his brother will be liable to judgment.

"You have heard that it was said, *You shall not commit adultery.* But I say to you, everyone who looks at a woman with lust has already committed adultery with her in his heart.

"Again you have heard that it was said to your ancestors,

Do not take a false oath,
but make good to the Lord all that you vow.

But I say to you, do not swear at all. Let your 'Yes' mean 'Yes,' and your 'No' mean 'No.' Anything more is from the evil one."

First Reading (Sir 15:15-20)

If you choose you can keep the commandments, they will save you;
    if you trust in God, you too shall live;
he has set before you fire and water;
    to whichever you choose, stretch forth your hand.
Before man are life and death, good and evil,
    whichever he chooses shall be given him.
Immense is the wisdom of the Lord;
    he is mighty in power, and all-seeing.
The eyes of God are on those who fear him;
    he understands man's every deed.
No one does he command to act unjustly,
    to none does he give license to sin.

Responsorial Psalm (Ps 119:1-2, 4-5, 17-18, 33-34)

℟. (1b) Blessed are they who follow the law of the Lord!

Blessed are they whose way is blameless,
  who walk in the law of the LORD.
Blessed are they who observe his decrees,
  who seek him with all their heart.

℟. Blessed are they who follow the law of the Lord!

You have commanded that your precepts
  be diligently kept.
Oh, that I might be firm in the ways
  of keeping your statutes!

℟. Blessed are they who follow the law of the Lord!

Be good to your servant, that I may live
  and keep your words.
Open my eyes, that I may consider
  the wonders of your law.

℟. Blessed are they who follow the law of the Lord!

Instruct me, O LORD, in the way of your statutes,
  that I may exactly observe them.
Give me discernment, that I may observe your law
  and keep it with all my heart.

℟. Blessed are they who follow the law of the Lord!

Second Reading (1 Cor 2:6-10)

Reflecting on Living the Gospel

What does it mean for Jesus to fulfill the law? Jesus sees in the law the means to the fulfillment of time, when the law will be replaced by righteous relationships within the kingdom of heaven. The fundamental law is gift of self to others. When self-giving is lacking in any act of keeping the law, the law in fact is not kept. We are to keep the law as the way to enter a manner of caring for and relating to others that leads to fullness of Life.

Connecting the Responsorial Psalm to the Readings

Psalm 119 is the longest psalm in the psalter and includes within its carefully planned framework many types of psalm genres all woven together in praise of God's law. The relationship between the verses of Psalm 119 selected for this responsorial psalm and the first reading and gospel are readily evident. Those who keep the commandments of God are choosing life over death, good over evil (first reading). Those who understand the deepest intent of the law see it not as a list of external rubrics but as an invitation to more just and loving relationships (gospel). In the psalm we ask God to give us the kind of discernment Jesus brings to the law. We pray also for the kind of obedience to the law Jesus exemplifies: obedience flowing from a heart tempered by compassion, forgiveness, truth, and mercy.

Psalmist Preparation

Wholehearted obedience to God's law leads not to a rigid heart but to a warm one. How have you grown over the years in your understanding of God's law? How has God's law made you more compassionate, more merciful, more truthful, more just? Where do you need to continue growing?

Prayer

God of the covenant, you give us the law that we may come to love you and one another more fully and freely. Lead us to live in our daily actions what your law has written in our hearts. We ask this through Christ our Lord. Amen.

Gospel (Matt 5:38-48; L79A)

Jesus said to his disciples: "You have heard that it was said,

An eye for an eye and a tooth for a tooth.

But I say to you, offer no resistance to one who is evil. When someone strikes you on your right cheek, turn the other one as well. If anyone wants to go to law with you over your tunic, hand over your cloak as well. Should anyone press you into service for one mile, go for two miles.

Give to the one who asks of you, and do not turn your back on one who wants to borrow.

"You have heard that it was said,

You shall love your neighbor and hate your enemy.

But I say to you, love your enemies and pray for those who persecute you, that you may be children of your heavenly Father, for he makes his sun rise on the bad and the good, and causes rain to fall on the just and the unjust. For if you love those who love you, what recompense will you have? Do not the tax collectors do the same? And if you greet your brothers only, what is unusual about that? Do not the pagans do the same? So be perfect, just as your heavenly Father is perfect."

First Reading (Lev 19:1-2, 17-18)

The LORD said to Moses, "Speak to the whole Israelite community and tell them: Be holy, for I, the LORD, your God, am holy.

"You shall not bear hatred for your brother or sister in your heart. Though you may have to reprove your fellow citizen, do not incur sin because of him. Take no revenge and cherish no grudge against any of your people. You shall love your neighbor as yourself. I am the LORD."

Responsorial Psalm (Ps 103:1-2, 3-4, 8, 10, 12-13)

℟. (8a) The Lord is kind and merciful.

Bless the LORD, O my soul;
　　and all my being, bless his holy name.
Bless the LORD, O my soul,
　　and forget not all his benefits.

R℣. The Lord is kind and merciful.

He pardons all your iniquities,
heals all your ills.
He redeems your life from destruction,
crowns you with kindness and compassion.

R℣. The Lord is kind and merciful.

Merciful and gracious is the LORD,
slow to anger and abounding in kindness.
Not according to our sins does he deal with us,
nor does he requite us according to our crimes.

R℣. The Lord is kind and merciful.

As far as the east is from the west,
so far has he put our transgressions from us.
As a father has compassion on his children,
so the LORD has compassion on those who fear him.

R℣. The Lord is kind and merciful.

Second Reading (1 Cor 3:16-23)

Reflecting on Living the Gospel

All our human actions are finite and limited, so even going the extra mile
is still just one more mile. Giving our coat to another is still just a coat.
Jesus is asking us to stop thinking in terms of measurements, and begin
acting in terms of how our heavenly Father treats us. God's graces are
showered upon all; God's care is extended to all; God's love is poured
forth upon all. But most of all, God's Son loved with his all. He showed
us what "perfect" is: he gave himself. Again and again.

Connecting the Responsorial Psalm to the Readings

We begin this responsorial psalm commanding our whole being to bless
God who pardons our sins, heals our ills, and redeems us from destruction. Rather than the justice our human hearts so readily understand and
measure out, our God offers us mercy far beyond our comprehension ("as
far as the east is from the west"). Such attitudes and actions describe the
holiness of God. Divine holiness is not an attribute but a state of being:
God *is* holy. And we are to be holy as God is (first reading), perfect as
God is (gospel). Jesus spells out the details. We are to relate to one another as God relates to us, going beyond the expected, loving without reserve, forgiving even what is unforgivable. Can we do this?

Psalmist Preparation

In singing this responsorial psalm you tell the assembly about the holiness of God, who is compassionate, merciful, and forgiving. This is the holiness to which they are called (see first reading and gospel). Where do you see this holiness in them? in yourself?

Prayer

Loving God, even when we do not deserve it, you treat us with mercy and compassion, understanding and forgiveness. Teach us to act toward one another as you act toward us that we may be holy like you. We ask this through Christ our Lord. Amen.

MARCH 2, 2014

Gospel (Matt 6:24-34; L82A)

Jesus said to his disciples: "No one can serve two masters. He will either hate one and love the other, or be devoted to one and despise the other. You cannot serve God and mammon.

"Therefore I tell you, do not worry about your life, what you will eat or drink, or about your body, what you will wear. Is not life more than food and the body more than clothing? Look at the birds in the sky; they do not sow or reap, they gather nothing into barns, yet your heavenly Father feeds them. Are not you more important than they? Can any of you by worrying add a single moment to your life-span? Why are you anxious about clothes? Learn from the way the wild flowers grow. They do not work or spin. But I tell you that not even Solomon in all his splendor was clothed like one of them. If God so clothes the grass of the field, which grows today and is thrown into the oven tomorrow,  will he not much more provide for you, O you of little faith? So do not worry and say, 'What are we to eat?' or 'What are we to drink?' or 'What are we to wear?' All these things the pagans seek. Your heavenly Father knows that you need them all. But seek first the kingdom of God and his righteousness, and all these things will be given you besides. Do not worry about tomorrow; tomorrow will take care of itself. Sufficient for a day is its own evil."

First Reading (Isa 49:14-15)

Zion said, "The LORD has forsaken me;
    my Lord has forgotten me."
Can a mother forget her infant,
    be without tenderness for the child of her womb?
Even should she forget,
    I will never forget you.

Responsorial Psalm (Ps 62:2-3, 6-7, 8-9)

℟. (6a) Rest in God alone, my soul.

Only in God is my soul at rest;
    from him comes my salvation.

He only is my rock and my salvation,
my stronghold; I shall not be disturbed at all.

℟. Rest in God alone, my soul.

Only in God be at rest, my soul,
for from him comes my hope.
He only is my rock and my salvation,
my stronghold; I shall not be disturbed.

℟. Rest in God alone, my soul.

With God is my safety and my glory,
he is the rock of my strength; my refuge is in God.
Trust in him at all times, O my people!
Pour out your hearts before him.

℟. Rest in God alone, my soul.

Second Reading (1 Cor 4:1-5)

Reflecting on Living the Gospel

Jesus is clear: "do not worry." Telling humans not to worry about tomorrow is like telling them not to be the center of their own lives. And that is exactly the point of this gospel! The two masters are God or ourselves. Yes, we ourselves are the mammon. If we choose ourselves, we worry. If we choose God, we will feed on God's generosity, be clothed in God's gift of Life, and be made rich in faith. This choice is sufficient not only for a day, but for a whole lifetime—even for all eternity.

Connecting the Responsorial Psalm to the Readings

The first reading, psalm, and gospel present us with the same message: we are not to worry about our well-being, for God is the rock of our salvation (psalm), the mother who will never forget us (first reading), and the father who will provide for our every need (gospel). Knowing this, Jesus chides us to put our priorities in order and pursue God's kingdom and God's righteousness above all other goods.

But doing this is not easy! Placing pursuit of God's kingdom above all other concerns requires immense trust in God. And this is precisely Jesus' point. He is calling us to see more clearly how intimately God is involved in our lives, both in its daily unfolding and in its ultimate outcome. He is inviting us to choose as master One who is our father, mother, rock, and refuge, One who perceives our deepest needs and never fails to fill them. We can "Rest in God alone" for everything we need will be given to us.

Psalmist Preparation

Your singing of this responsorial psalm needs to come from a heart and mind filled with confidence and trust in God. When are you most able to "rest in God"? What leads you to become restless and worried? How in the midst of worry do you refocus on God?

Prayer

Good and gracious God, you guard our present and protect our future, providing for our every need. Lead us to rest confidently in your care for us and to seek only your kingdom. We ask this through Christ our Lord. Amen.

Gospel (Matt 6:1-6, 16-18; L219)

Jesus said to his disciples: "Take care not to perform righteous deeds in order that people may see them; otherwise, you will have no recompense from your heavenly Father. When you give alms, do not blow a trumpet before you, as the hypocrites do in the synagogues and in the streets to win the praise of others. Amen, I say to you, they have received their reward. But when you give alms, do not let your left hand know what your right is doing, so that your almsgiving may be secret. And your Father who sees in secret will repay you.

"When you pray, do not be like the hypocrites, who love to stand and pray in the synagogues and on street corners so that others may see them. Amen, I say to you, they have received their reward. But when you pray, go to your inner room, close the door, and pray to your Father in secret. And your Father who sees in secret will repay you.

"When you fast, do not look gloomy like the hypocrites. They neglect their appearance, so that they may appear to others to be fasting. Amen, I say to you, they have received their reward. But when you fast, anoint your head and wash your face, so that you may not appear to be fasting, except to your Father who is hidden. And your Father who sees what is hidden will repay you."

First Reading (Joel 2:12-18)

Even now, says the LORD,
    return to me with your whole heart,
    with fasting, and weeping, and mourning;
Rend your hearts, not your garments,
    and return to the LORD, your God.
For gracious and merciful is he,
    slow to anger, rich in kindness,
    and relenting in punishment.
Perhaps he will again relent
    and leave behind him a blessing,
Offerings and libations
    for the LORD, your God.

Blow the trumpet in Zion!
    proclaim a fast,
    call an assembly;
Gather the people,
    notify the congregation;

Assemble the elders,
  gather the children
  and the infants at the breast;
Let the bridegroom quit his room
  and the bride her chamber.
Between the porch and the altar
  let the priests, the ministers of the LORD, weep,
And say, "Spare, O LORD, your people,
  and make not your heritage a reproach,
  with the nations ruling over them!
Why should they say among the peoples,
  'Where is their God?'"

Then the LORD was stirred to concern for his land and took pity on his people.

Responsorial Psalm (Ps 51:3-4, 5-6ab, 12-13, 14, and 17)

R♩. (see 3a) Be merciful, O Lord, for we have sinned.

Have mercy on me, O God, in your goodness;
  in the greatness of your compassion wipe out my offense.
Thoroughly wash me from my guilt
  and of my sin cleanse me.

R♩. Be merciful, O Lord, for we have sinned.

For I acknowledge my offense,
  and my sin is before me always:
"Against you only have I sinned,
  and done what is evil in your sight."

R♩. Be merciful, O Lord, for we have sinned.

A clean heart create for me, O God,
  and a steadfast spirit renew within me.
Cast me not out from your presence,
  and your Holy Spirit take not from me.

R♩. Be merciful, O Lord, for we have sinned.

Give me back the joy of your salvation,
  and a willing spirit sustain in me.
O Lord, open my lips,
  and my mouth shall proclaim your praise.

R♩. Be merciful, O Lord, for we have sinned.

See Appendix, p. 213, for Second Reading

Reflecting on Living the Gospel

Jesus tells us how *not* to "perform righteous deeds": not to do them to receive the praise of others and be immediately rewarded. He also tells us *how* to do Lenten penance: to do it "in secret" and receive lasting repayment from God. The heart of Lenten penance is the hard work of opening ourselves to God's transforming grace. This is internal work that bears external effects. What is to be seen is not the penance we do, but the fruit of penance: "the grace of God" (second reading) at work in us.

Connecting the Responsorial Psalm to the Readings

As we do every year, we begin our annual season of penance and transformation by singing Psalm 51. Of all the penitential psalms, Psalm 51 is the most open in its confession of sin and the most poignant in its plea for God's mercy. Psalm 51 takes us to that "secret" place (gospel) where we "rend our hearts" (first reading) so that God may change them (psalm). The good news is that God will do the cleansing work of transforming our inner selves (psalm). We have only to open our hearts and ask.

Psalmist Preparation

In singing Psalm 51 you acknowledge that you have not always been faithful and ask God to bring you back by re-creating your heart. You stand before the assembly as a living embodiment of both sides of the story of salvation: human sinfulness and divine mercy. Such witness demands a great deal of honesty and vulnerability. What can help you be honest before God? What can help you be vulnerable before the community?

Prayer

God of compassion, you embrace in mercy the sinner who returns to you with a contrite heart. Lead us through our Lenten practices of prayer, penance, and almsgiving to turn our hearts more fully toward you that we may rise transformed with new life on Easter. We ask this through Christ our Lord. Amen.

Gospel (Matt 4:1-11; L22A)

At that time Jesus was led by the Spirit into the desert to be tempted by the devil. He fasted for forty days and forty nights, and afterwards he was hungry. The tempter approached and said to him, "If you are the Son of God, command that these stones become loaves of bread." He said in reply, "It is written:

> *One does not live on bread alone,*
>   *but on every word that comes forth*
>   *from the mouth of God."*

Then the devil took him to the holy city, and made him stand on the parapet of the temple, and said to him, "If you are the Son of God, throw yourself down. For it is written:

> *He will command his angels*
>   *concerning you*
> *and with their hands they will*
>   *support you,*
> *lest you dash your foot against a stone."*

Jesus answered him, "Again it is written,

> *You shall not put the Lord, your God, to the test."*

Then the devil took him up to a very high mountain, and showed him all the kingdoms of the world in their magnificence, and he said to him, "All these I shall give to you, if you will prostrate yourself and worship me." At this, Jesus said to him, "Get away, Satan! It is written:

> *The Lord, your God, shall you worship*
>   *and him alone shall you serve."*

Then the devil left him and, behold, angels came and ministered to him.

First Reading (Gen 2:7-9; 3:1-7)

The Lord God formed man out of the clay of the ground and blew into his nostrils the breath of life, and so man became a living being.

Then the Lord God planted a garden in Eden, in the east, and placed there the man whom he had formed. Out of the ground the Lord God made various trees grow that were delightful to look at and good for food, with the tree of life in the middle of the garden and the tree of the knowledge of good and evil.

Now the serpent was the most cunning of all the animals that the LORD God had made. The serpent asked the woman, "Did God really tell you not to eat from any of the trees in the garden?" The woman answered the serpent: "We may eat of the fruit of the trees in the garden; it is only about the fruit of the tree in the middle of the garden that God said, 'You shall not eat it or even touch it, lest you die.'" But the serpent said to the woman: "You certainly will not die! No, God knows well that the moment you eat of it your eyes will be opened and you will be like gods who know what is good and what is evil." The woman saw that the tree was good for food, pleasing to the eyes, and desirable for gaining wisdom. So she took some of its fruit and ate it; and she also gave some to her husband, who was with her, and he ate it. Then the eyes of both of them were opened, and they realized that they were naked; so they sewed fig leaves together and made loincloths for themselves.

Responsorial Psalm (Ps 51:3-4, 5-6, 12-13, 17)

℞. (cf. 3a) Be merciful, O Lord, for we have sinned.

Have mercy on me, O God, in your goodness;
 in the greatness of your compassion wipe out my offense.
Thoroughly wash me from my guilt
 and of my sin cleanse me.

℞. Be merciful, O Lord, for we have sinned.

For I acknowledge my offense,
 and my sin is before me always:
"Against you only have I sinned,
 and done what is evil in your sight."

℞. Be merciful, O Lord, for we have sinned.

A clean heart create for me, O God,
 and a steadfast spirit renew within me.
Cast me not out from your presence,
 and your Holy Spirit take not from me.

℞. Be merciful, O Lord, for we have sinned.

Give me back the joy of your salvation,
  and a willing spirit sustain in me.
O Lord, open my lips,
  and my mouth shall proclaim your praise.
R̟/. Be merciful, O Lord, for we have sinned.

See Appendix, p. 213, for Second Reading

Reflecting on Living the Gospel

Jesus spent forty days alone in the desert and was vulnerable, so the devil tried to allure him with tantalizing temptations. Temptation is essentially an enticement to put our own desires and needs first. Resisting temptation, then, is really resisting self-centeredness. Like Jesus, we must choose instead to surrender ourselves to God who alone should be the center of our lives. To make any other choice is to choose a false god. This First Sunday of Lent poses this question: Do we serve god or God?

Connecting the Responsorial Psalm to the Readings

Psalm 51 is a most appropriate way for us to begin this Lenten season of penance and transformation. The second reading indicates that we participate in both *adam's* (Hebrew: humankind) tendency toward sinfulness and disobedience to God, and Christ's capacity for obedience and fidelity. Between this weakness (first reading) and this steadfastness (gospel) stands God's redeeming goodness and compassion (psalm). Psalm 51 is our honest admission of sin and our plea that God transform us so that we might participate more fully in the loving obedience of Jesus. We begin Lent, then, singing the theme song of our entire lives. May we sing it often and well.

Psalmist Preparation

In singing Psalm 51 you stand before the assembly as a living embodiment of both sides of the story of salvation: human sinfulness and divine mercy. Such witness demands a great deal of honesty and vulnerability. What can help you be honest before God? What can help you be vulnerable before the community?

Prayer

God of mercy, you embrace the sinner who returns to you. Forgive our wanderings from your path of goodness and grace and lead us back to the joy of your salvation. We ask this through Christ our Lord. Amen.

Gospel (Matt 17:1-9; L25A)

Jesus took Peter, James, and John his brother, and led them up a high mountain by themselves. And he was transfigured before them; his face shone like the sun and his clothes became white as light. And behold, Moses and Elijah appeared to them, conversing with him. Then Peter

said to Jesus in reply, "Lord, it is good that we are here. If you wish, I will make three tents here, one for you, one for Moses, and one for Elijah." While he was still speaking, behold, a bright cloud cast a shadow over them, then from the cloud came a voice that said, "This is my beloved Son, with whom I am well pleased; listen to him." When the disciples heard this, they fell prostrate and were very much afraid. But Jesus came and touched them, saying, "Rise, and do not be afraid." And when the disciples raised their eyes, they saw no one else but Jesus alone.

As they were coming down from the mountain, Jesus charged them, "Do not tell the vision to anyone until the Son of Man has been raised from the dead."

First Reading (Gen 12:1-4a)

The LORD said to Abram: "Go forth from the land of your kinsfolk and from your father's house to a land that I will show you.

"I will make of you a great nation,
  and I will bless you;
I will make your name great,
  so that you will be a blessing.
I will bless those who bless you
  and curse those who curse you.
All the communities of the earth
  shall find blessing in you."

Abram went as the LORD directed him.

Responsorial Psalm (Ps 33:4-5, 18-19, 20, 22)

℟. (22) Lord, let your mercy be on us, as we place our trust in you.

Upright is the word of the LORD,
  and all his works are trustworthy.
He loves justice and right;
  of the kindness of the LORD the earth is full.

℟. Lord, let your mercy be on us, as we place our trust in you.

See, the eyes of the LORD are upon those who fear him,
  upon those who hope for his kindness,
to deliver them from death
  and preserve them in spite of famine.

℟. Lord, let your mercy be on us, as we place our trust in you.

Our soul waits for the LORD,
  who is our help and our shield.
May your kindness, O LORD, be upon us
  who have put our hope in you.

℟. Lord, let your mercy be on us, as we place our trust in you.

See Appendix, p. 214, for Second Reading

Reflecting on Living the Gospel

What high mountain must we climb for us to witness Jesus' transfiguration? We must climb the high mountain of listening to Jesus, the high mountain of being pleasing to him, the high mountain of opening ourselves to the touch of his Presence. When we climb this mountain, we forsake our own agenda of pitching the tent where we choose and enter into the glory of the life Jesus offers us. The mountain is steep; the climb is ours to choose; the vision at the top is divine—"white as light," shining "like the sun." Can we see him?

Connecting the Responsorial Psalm to the Readings

Part of the "hardship" we bear as disciples (second reading) is that like Abram (first reading) we must leave behind what we know and love and journey into an unknown future. Part of the blessing of discipleship is that like Peter, James, and John in the gospel we are given glimpses along the way of the glory which is to come. Called to be faithful to the journey and strengthened along the way by flashes of glory, we live in the in-between time of hope.

Our hope, like Abram's, like Christ's, like the apostles, lies in the awareness that the One calling us forward will be faithful to the promise. Through the trudging and the temptations (last Sunday) we see this promise shining even now, fleeting but with overwhelming clarity (this Sunday). The promise of future glory is real and the merciful God who keeps a tender eye upon us (psalm) grants us visions of it so that we may keep moving onward.

Psalmist Preparation

As you sing these verses from Psalm 33 you express the hope fulfilled in the gospel reading. The unseen future to which Abram was called (first reading) is fully manifest in the shining face of Jesus on the mountaintop. You sing of the trust we can hold in the God who promises such a future to us. You are a beacon of hope to the assembly. How can you be this beacon also in your daily living to those who lack hope or need encouragement?

Prayer

Lord, as we travel our Lenten journey to the cross, grant us glimpses of the glory to which you are leading us so that we may walk with courage and persevere in hope. We ask this through Christ our Lord. Amen.

Gospel (John 4:5-42 [or shorter form below John 4:5-15, 19b-26, 39a, 40-42]; L28A)

Jesus came to a town of Samaria called Sychar, near the plot of land that Jacob had given to his son Joseph. Jacob's well was there. Jesus, tired from his journey, sat down there at the well. It was about noon.

A woman of Samaria came to draw water. Jesus said to her, "Give me a drink." His disciples had gone into the town to buy food. The Samaritan woman said to him, "How can you, a Jew, ask me, a Samaritan woman, for a drink?" —For Jews use nothing in common with Samaritans.— Jesus answered and said to her, "If you knew the gift of God and who is saying to you, 'Give me a drink,' you would have asked him and he would have given you living water." The woman said to him, "Sir, you do not even have a bucket and the cistern is deep; where then can you get this living water? Are you greater than our father Jacob, who gave us this cistern and drank from it himself with his children and his flocks?" Jesus answered and said to her, "Everyone who drinks this water will be thirsty again; but whoever drinks the water I shall give will never thirst; the water I shall give will become in him a spring of water welling up to eternal life." The woman said to him, "Sir, give me this water, so that I may not be thirsty or have to keep coming here to draw water."

"I can see that you are a prophet. Our ancestors worshiped on this mountain; but you people say that the place to worship is in Jerusalem." Jesus said to her, "Believe me, woman, the hour is coming when you will worship the Father neither on this mountain nor in Jerusalem. You people worship what you do not understand; we worship what we understand, because salvation is from the Jews. But the hour is coming, and is now here, when true worshipers will worship the Father in Spirit and truth; and indeed the Father seeks such people to worship him. God is Spirit, and those who worship him must worship in Spirit and truth." The woman said to him, "I know that the Messiah is coming, the one called the Christ; when he comes, he will tell us everything." Jesus said to her, "I am he, the one speaking with you."

Many of the Samaritans of that town began to believe in him. When the Samaritans came to him, they invited him to stay with them; and he stayed there two days. Many more began to believe in him because of his word, and they said to the woman, "We no longer believe because of your word; for we have heard for ourselves, and we know that this is truly the savior of the world."

First Reading (Exod 17:3-7)

In those days, in their thirst for water, the people grumbled against Moses, saying, "Why did you ever make us leave Egypt? Was it just to have us die here of thirst with our children and our livestock?" So Moses cried out to the LORD, "What shall I do with this people? A little more and they will stone me!" The LORD answered Moses, "Go over there in front of the people, along with some of the elders of Israel, holding in your hand, as you go, the staff with which you struck the river. I will be standing there in front of you on the rock in Horeb. Strike the rock, and the water will flow from it for the people to drink." This Moses did, in the presence of the elders of Israel. The place was called Massah and Meribah, because the Israelites quarreled there and tested the LORD, saying, "Is the LORD in our midst or not?"

Responsorial Psalm (Ps 95:1-2, 6-7, 8-9)

R℣. (8) If today you hear his voice, harden not your hearts.

Come, let us sing joyfully to the LORD;
    let us acclaim the Rock of our salvation.
Let us come into his presence with thanksgiving;
    let us joyfully sing psalms to him.

R℣. If today you hear his voice, harden not your hearts.

Come, let us bow down in worship;
    let us kneel before the LORD who made us.
For he is our God,
    and we are the people he shepherds, the flock he guides.

R℣. If today you hear his voice, harden not your hearts.

Oh, that today you would hear his voice:
    "Harden not your hearts as at Meribah,
    as in the day of Massah in the desert.
Where your fathers tempted me;
    they tested me though they had seen my works."

R℣. If today you hear his voice, harden not your hearts.

See Appendix, p. 214, for Second Reading

Reflecting on Living the Gospel

When Jesus asked the Samaritan woman for a drink of water, she completely misunderstood what Jesus was really asking: to understand the "gift of God" already given to her. What he was offering her was the gift of his very Self: the living water that would lead her from chance meeting to divine encounter, from being a woman who attempts to deceive Jesus to becoming one who gives true testimony to "the Christ," from her expectation of the Messiah to her belief that the "savior of the world" has come. True encounters with Jesus never leave anyone the same.

Connecting the Responsorial Psalm to the Readings

Psalm 95 begins by calling us to praise God, the "Rock of our salvation." The psalm then urges us to worship God, our shepherd. The end of the psalm makes a dramatic shift, however, warning us not to bicker with our shepherd God by claiming like the Israelites in the desert that God does not care for us (first reading).

Unlike the Israelites in the desert the Samaritan woman does not test Jesus but probes for better understanding of what he is saying (gospel). Once she grasps his meaning she runs immediately to tell others about him. Do we like her believe that Jesus is the living water? Do we believe that he will satisfy our thirst? When discipleship becomes difficult will we probe for deeper understanding, or will we complain that we do not have everything we want? Will we harden our hearts, or will we open our hearts to see in Christ the proof of God's love for us (second reading)?

Psalmist Preparation

Psalm 95 is a prophetic challenge. The first two strophes are easy to sing as you call the community to praise and worship God. The third strophe, however, is not so easy. How do you challenge the community's integrity? How do you call them to honest assessment of their fidelity? You can only do this with integrity if you have applied the psalm's message to yourself. When do you harden your heart against God? Why? Who challenges you to reopen your heart? How?

Prayer

Lord, help us drink deeply of the living water, Jesus, that we may come to know him more fully and walk more faithfully in his path of life. We ask this through Christ our Lord. Amen.

Gospel (John 9:1-41 [or shorter form below John 9:1, 6-9, 13-17, 34-38]; L31A)
As Jesus passed by he saw a man blind from birth. He spat on the ground and made clay with the saliva, and smeared the clay on his eyes, and said to him, "Go wash in the Pool of Siloam"—which means Sent—. So he went and washed, and came back able to see.

His neighbors and those who had seen him earlier as a beggar said, "Isn't this the one who used to sit and beg?" Some said, "It is," but others said, "No, he just looks like him." He said, "I am."

They brought the one who was once blind to the Pharisees. Now Jesus had made clay and opened his eyes on a sabbath. So then the Pharisees also asked him how he was able to see. He said to them, "He put clay on my eyes, and I washed, and now I can see." So some of the Pharisees said, "This man is not from God, because he does not keep the sabbath." But others said, "How can a sinful man do such signs?" And there was a division among them. So they said to the blind man again, "What do you have to say about him, since he opened your eyes?" He said, "He is a prophet."

They answered and said to him, "You were born totally in sin, and are you trying to teach us?" Then they threw him out.

When Jesus heard that they had thrown him out, he found him and said, "Do you believe in the Son of Man?" He answered and said, "Who is he, sir, that I may believe in him?" Jesus said to him, "You have seen him, and the one speaking with you is he." He said, "I do believe, Lord," and he worshiped him.

First Reading (1 Sam 16:1b, 6-7, 10-13a)
The LORD said to Samuel: "Fill your horn with oil, and be on your way. I am sending you to Jesse of Bethlehem, for I have chosen my king from among his sons."

As Jesse and his sons came to the sacrifice, Samuel looked at Eliab and thought, "Surely the LORD's anointed is here before him." But the LORD said to Samuel: "Do not judge from his appearance or from his lofty stature, because I have rejected him. Not as man sees does God see, because man sees the appearance but the LORD looks into the heart." In the same way Jesse presented seven sons before Samuel, but Samuel said to

Jesse, "The LORD has not chosen any one of these." Then Samuel asked Jesse, "Are these all the sons you have?" Jesse replied, "There is still the youngest, who is tending the sheep." Samuel said to Jesse, "Send for him; we will not begin the sacrificial banquet until he arrives here." Jesse sent and had the young man brought to them. He was ruddy, a youth handsome to behold and making a splendid appearance. The LORD said, "There—anoint him, for this is the one!" Then Samuel, with the horn of oil in hand, anointed David in the presence of his brothers; and from that day on, the spirit of the LORD rushed upon David.

***Responsorial Psalm* (Ps 23:1-3a, 3b-4, 5, 6)**

℟. (1) The Lord is my shepherd; there is nothing I shall want.

The LORD is my shepherd; I shall not want.
  In verdant pastures he gives me repose;
beside restful waters he leads me;
  he refreshes my soul.

℟. The Lord is my shepherd; there is nothing I shall want.

He guides me in right paths
  for his name's sake.
Even though I walk in the dark valley
  I fear no evil; for you are at my side
with your rod and your staff
  that give me courage.

℟. The Lord is my shepherd; there is nothing I shall want.

You spread the table before me
  in the sight of my foes;
you anoint my head with oil;
  my cup overflows.

℟. The Lord is my shepherd; there is nothing I shall want.

Only goodness and kindness follow me
  all the days of my life;
and I shall dwell in the house of the LORD
  for years to come.

℟. The Lord is my shepherd; there is nothing I shall want.

See Appendix, p. 214, for Second Reading

Reflecting on Living the Gospel

In making clay from his own saliva and smearing it on the blind man's eyes, Jesus re-creates the man by transferring something of his own being to the man. The man is anointed by Jesus as "I am" and comes to be a stalwart, believing disciple. Not even the powerful Pharisees can sway him from his testimony to the work of Jesus in him. In baptism we, too, encounter Jesus and become a new creation in him. Are we as stalwart and believing as the blind man?

Connecting the Responsorial Psalm to the Readings

Samuel anoints David (first reading), Jesus anoints the eyes of the blind man (gospel), our shepherd God anoints us (psalm). In all three anointings a new sense of identity is given: David becomes king, the blind man becomes a believer, we become members of God's household. Moreover, it is always God who seeks out the one to be anointed. God sends Samuel to find David, Jesus sees the blind man as he passes by and later seeks him out, Christ comes with light while we are hidden in darkness (second reading).

We, however, must choose the light Christ brings (second reading). Will we choose, like the Pharisees, not to see? Will we undergo the change in identity to which the seeing invites us? Will we stand by what we have seen even when we face opposition? The good news of the psalm is that Christ will shepherd us even while we struggle with darkness in ourselves and in others. We can walk the journey into light because Christ gives us the protection and courage we need.

Psalmist Preparation

After Jesus heals the blind man in this gospel story he leaves him to stand on his own before the ire of the temple authorities. Nonetheless, Jesus knows what is happening and seeks the man out when his ordeal is over. Even in seeming absence, then, the shepherd God about whom you sing in this psalm watches over you. This shepherd God does not shield you from the cost of discipleship, but trusts your ability to deal with it. At what difficult points in life has God seemed absent from you? How have these experiences strengthened your sense of God's confidence in you? Who or what has helped you discover this hidden confidence?

Prayer

God our shepherd, free us from the darkness of stubborn self-will and lead us to the light of your Son, Jesus, that we may walk with him along the path of life. We ask this through Christ our Lord. Amen.

Gospel (John 11:1-45 [or shorter form below John 11:3-7, 17, 20-27, 33b-45]; L34A)

The sisters of Lazarus sent word to Jesus saying, "Master, the one you love is ill." When Jesus heard this he said, "This illness is not to end in death, but is for the glory of God, that the Son of God may be glorified through it." Now Jesus loved Martha and her sister and Lazarus. So when he heard that he was ill, he remained for two days in the place where he was. Then after this he said to his disciples, "Let us go back to Judea."

When Jesus arrived, he found that Lazarus had already been in the tomb for four days. When Martha heard that Jesus was coming, she went to meet him; but Mary sat at home. Martha said to Jesus, "Lord, if you had been here, my brother would not have died. But even now I know that whatever you ask of God, God will give you." Jesus said to her, "Your brother will rise." Martha said, "I know he will rise, in the resurrection on the last day." Jesus told her, "I am the resurrection and the life; whoever believes in me, even if he dies, will live, and everyone who lives and believes in me will never die. Do you believe this?" She said to him, "Yes, Lord. I have come to believe that you are the Christ, the Son of God, the one who is coming into the world."

He became perturbed and deeply troubled, and said, "Where have you laid him?" They said to him, "Sir, come and see." And Jesus wept. So the Jews said, "See how he loved him." But some of them said, "Could not the one who opened the eyes of the blind man have done something so that this man would not have died?"

So Jesus, perturbed again, came to the tomb. It was a cave, and a stone lay across it. Jesus said, "Take away the stone." Martha, the dead man's sister, said to him, "Lord, by now there will be a stench; he has been dead for four days." Jesus said to her, "Did I not tell you that if you believe you will see the glory of God?" So they took away the stone. And Jesus raised his eyes and said, "Father, I thank you for hearing me. I know that you always hear me; but because of the crowd here I have said this, that they may believe that you sent me." And when he had said this, he cried out in a loud voice, "Lazarus, come

out!" The dead man came out, tied hand and foot with burial bands, and his face was wrapped in a cloth. So Jesus said to them, "Untie him and let him go."

Now many of the Jews who had come to Mary and seen what he had done began to believe in him.

First Reading (Ezek 37:12-14)

Thus says the Lord GOD: O my people, I will open your graves and have you rise from them, and bring you back to the land of Israel. Then you shall know that I am the LORD, when I open your graves and have you rise from them, O my people! I will put my spirit in you that you may live, and I will settle you upon your land; thus you shall know that I am the LORD. I have promised, and I will do it, says the LORD.

Responsorial Psalm (Ps 130:1-2, 3-4, 5-6, 7-8)

R̞. (7) With the Lord there is mercy and fullness of redemption.

Out of the depths I cry to you, O LORD;
> LORD, hear my voice!
Let your ears be attentive
> to my voice in supplication.

R̞. With the Lord there is mercy and fullness of redemption.

If you, O LORD, mark iniquities,
> LORD, who can stand?
But with you is forgiveness,
> that you may be revered.

R̞. With the Lord there is mercy and fullness of redemption.

I trust in the LORD;
> my soul trusts in his word.
More than sentinels wait for the dawn,
> let Israel wait for the LORD.

R̞. With the Lord there is mercy and fullness of redemption.

For with the LORD is kindness
> and with him is plenteous redemption;
and he will redeem Israel
> from all their iniquities.

R̞. With the Lord there is mercy and fullness of redemption.

See Appendix, p. 214, for Second Reading

Reflecting on Living the Gospel
Both Martha and Mary express great conviction in Jesus' healing power: "Lord, if you had been here, my brother would not have died." Their conviction, however, was tied to their human experience of the fragility of sickness and the finality of death. Jesus' action surpasses human experience and reveals something entirely new: "everyone who lives and believes in me will never die." Belief in Jesus unties us from the limits of human experience and frees us for the eternity of risen Life.

Connecting the Responsorial Psalm to the Readings
Psalm 130 is an individual lament arising from some unnamed anguish so profound that the psalmist feels buried in the bowels of the earth. There is some sense that the underlying cause of the anguish, indeed of all human anguish, is sin. If God were to tally our sins we would never rise from the pit. Because God does not tally sin but forgives it, however, the psalmist has hope. God's kindness is greater than Israel's iniquities; redemption is assured. We have only to wait.

And for what do we wait? The redemption not only of our souls, but of our bodies, promised metaphorically in the first reading, foreseen in the future in the second, and experienced here-and-now in the gospel when Jesus calls Lazarus forth from the tomb. The closer Jesus moves to his own death in Jerusalem, the more clearly he reveals his power over death. The closer we move to Jesus, the more we rise from the pit. In him the mercy of God is made flesh and our hope of redemption is made real.

Psalmist Preparation
The depth of hope you express in singing Psalm 130 will be determined by the depth of your experience of human anguish, both your own and that of the whole world. Ask Christ for a heart wide enough to contain this, compassionate enough to weep over it, and trusting enough to count on God to turn suffering and death into redemption and new Life.

Prayer
God of life, when death seems to be the final word, open our hearts to hear the Word Jesus calling us out of the tomb to new Life. We ask this through Christ our Lord. Amen.

PALM SUNDAY
OF THE PASSION OF THE LORD

Gospel at the procession with palms (Matt 21:1-11; L37A)

Gospel at the Mass (Matt 26:14–27:66; L38A)

First Reading (Isa 50:4-7)

The Lord GOD has given me
    a well-trained tongue,
that I might know how to speak to the weary
    a word that will rouse them.
Morning after morning
    he opens my ear that I may hear;
and I have not rebelled,
    have not turned back.
I gave my back to those who beat
      me,
    my cheeks to those who plucked
      my beard;
my face I did not shield
    from buffets and spitting.

The Lord GOD is my help,
    therefore I am not disgraced;
I have set my face like flint,
    knowing that I shall not be put to shame.

Responsorial Psalm (Ps 22:8-9, 17-18, 19-20, 23-24)

℟. (2a) My God, my God, why have you abandoned me?

All who see me scoff at me;
    they mock me with parted lips, they wag their heads:
"He relied on the LORD; let him deliver him,
    let him rescue him, if he loves him."

℟. My God, my God, why have you abandoned me?

Indeed, many dogs surround me,
    a pack of evildoers closes in upon me;
they have pierced my hands and my feet;
    I can count all my bones.

℟. My God, my God, why have you abandoned me?

They divide my garments among them,
    and for my vesture they cast lots.

But you, O L𝑜ʀᴅ, be not far from me;
O my help, hasten to aid me.

℞. My God, my God, why have you abandoned me?

I will proclaim your name to my brethren;
in the midst of the assembly I will praise you:
"You who fear the L𝑜ʀᴅ, praise him;
all you descendants of Jacob, give glory to him;
revere him, all you descendants of Israel!"

℞. My God, my God, why have you abandoned me?

See Appendix, p. 215, for Second Reading

Reflecting on Living the Gospel

Jesus warns the disciples at the Last Supper that their faith would be shaken, but the disciples deny that this will ever happen. Nonetheless, faith is greatly threatened when there is great cost and we instinctively protect ourselves. Jesus alone remains unshaken in his faith: in the Garden he says yes to his Father's will, he is silent before his accusers' false accusations, he willingly gives up his spirit on the cross. Instead of protecting himself, Jesus embraces the cost of his suffering and death—the great sign of his own faithfulness.

Connecting the Responsorial Psalm to the Readings

These verses from Psalm 22 move us from the glory of Jesus' triumphal entry into Jerusalem to the degradation of his passion: from hosannas to scoffing, from cheering crowds to ravening dogs and evildoers, from palms waved in honor to clothing stripped in humiliation. Yet the psalmist continues to praise God and to call the people to give God glory.

In the midst of his passion, Jesus likewise gives praise to God and calls us to give God glory. In response, God exalts him (second reading). The readings and psalm ask us, then, to reflect about where the real shouts of glory come from and what they are about. Not about the world's prizes. Not about fame and acclaim. But about obedience to God's will for human salvation. Because salvation entails dying, we, like Jesus, may well feel bereft and abandoned. But Jesus reveals that in the very dying itself God is there, upholding us and giving us glory.

Psalmist Preparation

In singing these verses from Psalm 22, you model for others both your willingness to enter with Christ into the suffering and death of the paschal mystery and your ability to sing God's praise as you do so. Pray this week that God will give you a "well-trained tongue" (first reading) able to offer praise in the midst of the suffering and death necessary for salvation. Pray that you—and everyone in the assembly—will be as united with Christ in his glory as you are with him in his dying.

Prayer

Redeeming God, you sent your Son to teach us to overcome death by willingly accepting it for the sake of others. Be with us as we enter this holiest week of the year. Give us the courage we need to walk with Jesus to the cross and to the glory beyond. We ask this through Christ our Lord. Amen.

APRIL 17, 2014

Gospel (John 13:1-15; L39ABC)

Before the feast of Passover, Jesus knew that his hour had come to pass from this world to the Father. He loved his own in the world and he loved them to the end. The devil had already induced Judas, son of Simon the Iscariot, to hand him over. So, during supper, fully aware that the Father had put everything into his power and that he had come from God and was returning to God, he rose from supper and took off his outer garments. He took a towel and tied it around his waist. Then he poured water into a basin and began to wash the disciples' feet and dry them with the towel around his waist. He came to Simon Peter, who said to him, "Master, are you going to wash my feet?" Jesus answered and said to him, "What I am doing, you do not understand now, but you will understand later." Peter said to him, "You will never wash my feet." Jesus answered him, "Unless I wash you, you will have no inheritance with me." Simon Peter said to him, "Master, then not only my feet, but my hands and head as well." Jesus said to him, "Whoever has bathed has no need except to have his feet washed, for he is clean all over; so you are clean, but not all." For he knew who would betray him; for this reason, he said, "Not all of you are clean."

So when he had washed their feet and put his garments back on and reclined at table again, he said to them, "Do you realize what I have done for you? You call me 'teacher' and 'master,' and rightly so, for indeed I am. If I, therefore, the master and teacher, have washed your feet, you ought to wash one another's feet. I have given you a model to follow, so that as I have done for you, you should also do."

First Reading (Exod 12:1-8, 11-14)

The LORD said to Moses and Aaron in the land of Egypt, "This month shall stand at the head of your calendar; you shall reckon it the first month of the year. Tell the whole community of Israel: On the tenth of this month every one of your families must procure for itself a lamb, one apiece for each household. If a family is too small for a whole lamb, it shall join the nearest household in procuring one and shall share in the lamb in proportion to the number of persons who partake of it. The lamb must be a year-old male and without blemish. You may take it from either the sheep or the goats. You shall keep it until the fourteenth day of this month, and then, with the whole assembly of Israel present, it shall be slaughtered during the evening twilight. They shall take some of its blood and apply it to the two doorposts and the lintel of every house in which they partake of the lamb. That same night they shall eat its roasted flesh with unleavened bread and bitter herbs.

"This is how you are to eat it: with your loins girt, sandals on your feet and your staff in hand, you shall eat like those who are in flight. It is the Passover of the LORD. For on this same night I will go through Egypt, striking down every firstborn of the land, both man and beast, and executing judgment on all the gods of Egypt—I, the LORD! But the blood will mark the houses where you are. Seeing the blood, I will pass over you; thus, when I strike the land of Egypt, no destructive blow will come upon you.

"This day shall be a memorial feast for you, which all your generations shall celebrate with pilgrimage to the LORD, as a perpetual institution."

Responsorial Psalm (Ps 116:12-13, 15-16bc, 17-18)

R℣. (cf. 1 Cor 10:16) Our blessing-cup is a communion with the Blood of Christ.

How shall I make a return to the LORD
    for all the good he has done for me?
The cup of salvation I will take up,
    and I will call upon the name of the LORD.

R℣. Our blessing-cup is a communion with the Blood of Christ.

Precious in the eyes of the LORD
    is the death of his faithful ones.
I am your servant, the son of your handmaid;
    you have loosed my bonds.

R℣. Our blessing-cup is a communion with the Blood of Christ.

To you will I offer sacrifice of thanksgiving,
    and I will call upon the name of the LORD.
My vows to the LORD I will pay
    in the presence of all his people.

R℣. Our blessing-cup is a communion with the Blood of Christ.

See Appendix, p. 215, for Second Reading

Reflecting on Living the Gospel

This night is about an eternity of self-giving. When Jesus asked his disciples, "Do you realize what I have done for you?" he was talking about much more than washing feet. He was talking about how God's glory is manifested: caring for others, paying attention to others, giving oneself to others. What glory is there in self-giving? The glory lies in making visible God's love.

Connecting the Responsorial Psalm to the Readings

The "blessing-cup" about which we sing in the psalm refrain was the third cup drunk as part of the Jewish Passover meal. Those who shared this cup were united with each other and God. On Holy Thursday—and at every celebration of the Eucharist—the "blessing-cup" we drink is the Blood of Christ, source of our salvation. By drinking this cup we take the Blood of Christ into ourselves and become one with him in his death and resurrection. Drinking this cup does not save us *from* death but *through* death, a death freely chosen in self-giving service to one another (gospel). By drinking it we not only "proclaim the death of the Lord" (second reading), we unite ourselves with him, and with one another, in his death, and find salvation.

Psalmist Preparation

What are the "vows to the Lord" you pay in drinking the blessing-cup of Christ's Blood? Certainly, you thank God for saving your life through Christ. But you also promise to become one with Christ in losing your life for the sake of others. You promise to become the servant who washes feet. Are you willing to do this? Whose feet need washing?

Prayer

God, you call us to communion in the Blood of Christ. May our drinking of his cup lead us always to serve one another in generous and joyful love. We ask this through Christ our Lord. Amen.

Gospel (John 18:1–19:42; L40ABC)

First Reading (Isa 52:13–53:12)

See, my servant shall prosper,
    he shall be raised high and greatly exalted.
Even as many were amazed at him—
    so marred was his look beyond human semblance
    and his appearance beyond that of the sons of man—
so shall he startle many nations,
    because of him kings shall stand speechless;
        for those who have not been told shall see,
          those who have not heard shall ponder it.

        Who would believe what we have heard?
          To whom has the arm of the LORD been
            revealed?
        He grew up like a sapling before him,
          like a shoot from the parched earth;
        there was in him no stately bearing to make
          us look at him,
          nor appearance that would attract us
           to him.
        He was spurned and avoided by people,
          a man of suffering, accustomed to
           infirmity,
one of those from whom people hide their faces,
    spurned, and we held him in no esteem.

Yet it was our infirmities that he bore,
    our sufferings that he endured,
while we thought of him as stricken,
    as one smitten by God and afflicted.
But he was pierced for our offenses,
    crushed for our sins;
upon him was the chastisement that makes us whole,
    by his stripes we were healed.
We had all gone astray like sheep,
    each following his own way;
but the LORD laid upon him
    the guilt of us all.

Though he was harshly treated, he submitted
    and opened not his mouth;
like a lamb led to the slaughter
    or a sheep before the shearers,
    he was silent and opened not his mouth.
Oppressed and condemned, he was taken away,
    and who would have thought any more of his destiny?
When he was cut off from the land of the living,
    and smitten for the sin of his people,
a grave was assigned him among the wicked
    and a burial place with evildoers,
though he had done no wrong
    nor spoken any falsehood.
But the LORD was pleased
    to crush him in infirmity.

If he gives his life as an offering for sin,
    he shall see his descendants in a long life,
    and the will of the LORD shall be accomplished through him.

Because of his affliction
    he shall see the light
        in fullness of days;
through his suffering, my servant shall justify many,
    and their guilt he shall bear.
Therefore I will give him his portion among the great,
    and he shall divide the spoils with the mighty,
because he surrendered himself to death
    and was counted among the wicked;
and he shall take away the sins of many,
    and win pardon for their offenses.

Responsorial Psalm (Ps 31:2, 6, 12-13, 15-16, 17, 25)

R℣. (Luke 23:46) Father, into your hands I commend my spirit.

In you, O LORD, I take refuge;
    let me never be put to shame.
In your justice rescue me.
    Into your hands I commend my spirit;
you will redeem me, O LORD, O faithful God.

R℣. Father, into your hands I commend my spirit.

For all my foes I am an object of reproach,
  a laughingstock to my neighbors, and a dread to my friends;
  they who see me abroad flee from me.
I am forgotten like the unremembered dead;
  I am like a dish that is broken.

R̸. Father, into your hands I commend my spirit.

But my trust is in you, O LORD;
  I say, "You are my God.
In your hands is my destiny; rescue me
  from the clutches of my enemies and my persecutors."

R̸. Father, into your hands I commend my spirit.

Let your face shine upon your servant;
  save me in your kindness.
Take courage and be stouthearted,
  all you who hope in the LORD.

R̸. Father, into your hands I commend my spirit.

See Appendix, p. 215, for Second Reading

Reflecting on Living the Gospel

Unlike Jesus, we do not carry our cross alone; we always have the support of the other members of the Body of Christ. Most importantly, we have the Presence, care, and love of the self-giving Jesus with us at all times, encouraging us and strengthening us in our own hour of need. We have Jesus' model of dignity and self-surrender. Jesus shows us how in all the simple acts of our everyday living we manifest the glory of the cross.

Connecting the Responsorial Psalm to the Readings

Psalm 31 is a poignant lament in which someone persecuted by enemies calls trustfully to God for help and then sings thanksgiving to God for salvation. Onlookers consider this person a fool ("laughingstock"), fearful to look at ("a dread"), someone best "forgotten." But to God this person is a faithful servant for whom God will always be the faithful redeemer. The Lectionary places words from Psalm 31 on the lips of Jesus, and frames his prayer with the refrain: "Father, into your hands I commend my spirit." Jesus' "spirit" is both his life-breath and the orientation of his heart. Amidst the unspeakable sufferings of his passion and death he continues to surrender himself, as he did all his life, to the Father in whose presence and care he trusts. The final verse stands as Jesus' words to us, and our words to all who remain faithful to God no matter what the personal cost: "Take courage . . . hope in the LORD."

Psalmist Preparation
You sing these words from Psalm 31 as one united with Jesus in his gift of self to the Father. In your singing you invite assembly members also to join themselves with Jesus. You encourage them in the final verse to remain "stouthearted" in their hope in the God of life and salvation. What keeps you stouthearted? How at this moment in your life do you need to give yourself over in obedience and trust to God? What gives you the courage to do so?

Prayer
God of salvation, in the life, death, and resurrection of your Son Jesus, you give over your Spirit to us. Open our hearts that, united with Jesus, we may return your gift by offering our spirit to you in obedience, trust, and love. We ask this through Christ our Lord. Amen.

Additional readings can be found in the Lectionary for Mass.

Gospel (Matt 28:1-10; L41ABC)

After the sabbath, as the first day of the week was dawning, Mary Magdalene and the other Mary came to see the tomb. And behold, there was a great earthquake; for an angel of the Lord descended from heaven, approached, rolled back the stone, and sat upon it. His appearance was like lightning and his clothing was white as snow. The guards were shaken with fear of him and became like dead men. Then the angel said to the women in reply, "Do not be afraid! I know that you are seeking Jesus the crucified. He is not here, for he has been raised just as he said. Come and see the place where he lay. Then go quickly and tell his disciples, 'He has been raised from the dead, and he is going before you to Galilee; there you will see him.' Behold, I have told you." Then they went away quickly from the tomb, fearful yet overjoyed, and ran to announce this to his disciples. And behold, Jesus met them on their way and greeted them. They approached, embraced his feet, and did him homage. Then Jesus said to them, "Do not be afraid. Go tell my brothers to go to Galilee, and there they will see me."

Epistle (Rom 6:3-11)

Brothers and sisters: Are you unaware that we who were baptized into Christ Jesus were baptized into his death? We were indeed buried with him through baptism into death, so that, just as Christ was raised from the dead by the glory of the Father, we too might live in newness of life.

For if we have grown into union with him through a death like his, we shall also be united with him in the resurrection. We know that our old self was crucified with him, so that our sinful body might be done away with, that we might no longer be in slavery to sin. For a dead person has been absolved from sin. If, then, we have died with Christ, we believe that we shall also live with him. We know that Christ, raised from the dead, dies no more; death no longer has power over him. As to his death, he died to sin once and for all; as to his life, he lives for God. Consequently, you too must think of yourselves as being dead to sin and living for God in Christ Jesus.

Responsorial Psalm (Ps 118:1-2, 16-17, 22-23)

R⁊. Alleluia, alleluia, alleluia.

Give thanks to the LORD, for he is good,
    for his mercy endures forever.
Let the house of Israel say,
    "His mercy endures forever."

R⁊. Alleluia, alleluia, alleluia.

The right hand of the LORD has struck with power;
    the right hand of the LORD is exalted.
I shall not die, but live,
    and declare the works of the LORD.

R⁊. Alleluia, alleluia, alleluia.

The stone which the builders rejected
    has become the cornerstone.
By the LORD has this been done;
    it is wonderful in our eyes.

R⁊. Alleluia, alleluia, alleluia.

Reflecting on Living the Gospel

This night is like no other. Each year we confront the power of darkness and rejoice with the bursting forth of Life. This is the night for which we have been preparing all Lent. This is the night when we celebrate Christ's victory over death and pledge ourselves in our renewal of baptismal promises to model our lives after him. This is the night when glory shines forth like lightning and is dazzling as snow. This is the night when Jesus' risen Life is announced. This is the night when encounter with Jesus imbues us with his risen Life.

Connecting the Responsorial Psalm to the Readings

Psalm 118 was a hymn sung as the Israelites processed into the temple to give thanks to God for saving them from destruction by an enemy. The procession entailed a march through the streets during which a soloist sang verses about facing death and a choir responded with verses about God's intervention to save. Verses 14, 15-16 are drawn from Exodus 15, indicating the Israelites saw every victory over an enemy as an extension of the Exodus event when God led them from slavery to freedom.

Psalm 118 is also our song of deliverance. Our saving event comes in Christ with whom we have died and risen, and with whom we share glory (Epistle). Our call is to believe what has happened to Christ (gospel) and become aware of what has happened to us (Epistle). As we sing Psalm 118, Christ is the soloist leading the song and we are the ones answering "Alleluia!"

Psalmist Preparation

Are you unaware that you have died and risen with Christ (see Epistle)? You proclaim to the assembly the wonderful work done by God in Christ and also done in them. How might you communicate the joy you feel this day both for yourself and for them?

Prayer

Saving God, you raise us out of the darkness of sin and death to new Life in your Son. May we always declare your saving works and live fully aware of what you have achieved in us. We ask this through Christ our Lord. Amen.

Gospel (John 20:1-9; L42ABC)

On the first day of the week, Mary of Magdala came to the tomb early in the morning, while it was still dark, and saw the stone removed from the tomb. So she ran and went to Simon Peter and to the other disciple whom Jesus loved, and told them, "They have taken the Lord from the tomb, and we don't know where they put him." So Peter and the other disciple went out and came to the tomb. They both ran, but the other disciple ran faster than Peter and arrived at the tomb first; he bent down and saw the burial cloths there, but did not go in. When Simon Peter arrived after him, he went into the tomb and saw the burial cloths there, and the cloth that had covered his head, not with the burial cloths but rolled up in a separate place. Then the other disciple also went in, the one who had arrived at the tomb first, and he saw and believed. For they did not yet understand the Scripture that he had to rise from the dead.

or Gospel (Matt 28:1-10; L41A)

**or at an afternoon or evening Mass
Gospel (Luke 24:13-35; L46)**

First Reading (Acts 10:34a, 37-43)

Peter proceeded to speak and said: "You know what has happened all over Judea, beginning in Galilee after the baptism that John preached, how God anointed Jesus of Nazareth with the Holy Spirit and power.

He went about doing good and healing all those oppressed by the devil, for God was with him. We are witnesses of all that he did both in the country of the Jews and in Jerusalem. They put him to death by hanging him on a tree. This man God raised on the third day and granted that he be visible, not to all the people, but to us, the witnesses chosen by God in advance, who ate and drank with him after he rose from the dead. He commissioned us to preach to the people and testify that he is the one appointed by God as judge of the living and the dead. To him all the prophets bear witness, that everyone who believes in him will receive forgiveness of sins through his name."

Responsorial Psalm (Ps 118:1-2, 16-17, 22-23)

R︎. (24) This is the day the Lord has made; let us rejoice and be glad.
or: R︎. Alleluia.

Give thanks to the LORD, for he is good,
for his mercy endures forever.
Let the house of Israel say,
"His mercy endures forever."

R︎. This is the day the Lord has made; let us rejoice and be glad.
or: R︎. Alleluia.

"The right hand of the LORD has struck with power;
the right hand of the LORD is exalted.
I shall not die, but live,
and declare the works of the LORD."

R︎. This is the day the Lord has made; let us rejoice and be glad.
or: R︎. Alleluia.

The stone which the builders rejected
has become the cornerstone.
By the LORD has this been done;
it is wonderful in our eyes.

R︎. This is the day the Lord has made; let us rejoice and be glad.
or: R︎. Alleluia.

See Appendix, p. 216, for Second Reading

Reflecting on Living the Gospel
Mary went to the tomb "early in the morning while it was still dark." When she arrived, she saw the stone rolled back and nothing but emptiness, no doubt reinforcing the darkness of sadness and loss in her heart. It would take an encounter with the risen One for her and the other disciples to understand that Jesus had risen. And then their darkness would give way to glory, to light, to Life, to believing, to unmitigated joy. Emptiness would become fullness. He has risen!

Connecting the Responsorial Psalm to the Readings
Psalm 118 was a hymn sung as the Israelites processed into the temple to give thanks to God for saving them from destruction by an enemy. The procession entailed a march through the streets during which a soloist

sang verses about facing death and a choir responded with verses about God's intervention to save. Verses 14, 15-16 are drawn from Exodus 15, indicating the Israelites saw every victory over an enemy as an extension of the Exodus event when God led them from slavery to freedom.

Psalm 118 is also our song of deliverance. Our saving event comes in Christ with whom we have died and risen, and with whom we share glory (second reading from Colossians). Our mission is to proclaim this work of God to all peoples (first reading). In singing Psalm 118 we do just that, calling all to rejoice in God's wonderful deeds.

Psalmist Preparation

In Psalm 118, the source of the responsorial psalm for Easter Sunday, a choir led the Israelites processing into the temple in their praise for God's mighty acts of salvation. This is your role, not only on Easter but every Sunday. In order to sing of God's saving deeds, however, you must know what they are. How have you experienced death and resurrection this Lent? How has your family experienced it? your parish? the world?

Prayer

All-powerful God, you raised your Son Jesus from the darkness of the tomb to the brightness of new Life. Keep us united with him so that we, too, may be raised from death to new Life. We ask this through Christ our Lord. Amen.

Gospel (John 20:19-31; L43A)

On the evening of that first day of the week, when the doors were locked, where the disciples were, for fear of the Jews, Jesus came and stood in their midst and said to them, "Peace be with you." When he had said this, he showed them his hands and his side. The disciples rejoiced when they saw the Lord. Jesus said to them again, "Peace be with you. As the Father has sent me, so I send you." And when he had said this, he breathed on them and said to them, "Receive the Holy Spirit. Whose sins you forgive are forgiven them, and whose sins you retain are retained."

Thomas, called Didymus, one of the Twelve, was not with them when Jesus came. So the other disciples said to him, "We have seen the Lord." But he said to them, "Unless I see the mark of the nails in his hands and put my finger into the nailmarks and put my hand into his side, I will not believe."

Now a week later his disciples were again inside and Thomas was with them. Jesus came, although the doors were locked, and stood in their midst and said, "Peace be with you." Then he said to Thomas, "Put your finger here and see my hands, and bring your hand and put it into my side, and do not be unbelieving, but believe." Thomas answered and said to him, "My Lord and my God!" Jesus said to him, "Have you come to believe because you have seen me? Blessed are those who have not seen and have believed."

Now Jesus did many other signs in the presence of his disciples that are not written in this book. But these are written that you may come to believe that Jesus is the Christ, the Son of God, and that through this belief you may have life in his name.

First Reading (Acts 2:42-47)

They devoted themselves to the teaching of the apostles and to the communal life, to the breaking of bread and to the prayers. Awe came upon everyone, and many wonders and signs were done through the apostles. All who believed were together and had all things in common; they would sell their property and possessions and divide them among all according to each one's need. Every day they devoted themselves to meeting together in the temple area and to breaking bread in their homes. They ate their meals with exultation and sincerity of heart, praising God and enjoying favor with all the people. And every day the Lord added to their number those who were being saved.

Responsorial Psalm (Ps 118:2-4, 13-15, 22-24)

R̶J̶. (1) Give thanks to the Lord for he is good, his love is everlasting.
or: R̶J̶. Alleluia.

Let the house of Israel say,
"His mercy endures forever."
Let the house of Aaron say,
"His mercy endures forever."
Let those who fear the LORD say,
"His mercy endures forever."

R̶J̶. Give thanks to the Lord for he is good, his love is everlasting.
or: R̶J̶. Alleluia.

I was hard pressed and was falling,
but the LORD helped me.
My strength and my courage is the LORD,
and he has been my savior.
The joyful shout of victory
in the tents of the just.

R̶J̶. Give thanks to the Lord for he is good, his love is everlasting.
or: R̶J̶. Alleluia.

The stone which the builders rejected
has become the cornerstone.
By the LORD has this been done;
it is wonderful in our eyes.
This is the day the LORD has made;
let us be glad and rejoice in it.

R̶J̶. Give thanks to the Lord for he is good, his love is everlasting.
or: R̶J̶. Alleluia.

See Appendix, p. 216, for Second Reading

Reflecting on Living the Gospel

The basic issue in this gospel story is coming to believe that Jesus is risen and alive. Believing is not dependent on physical contact with Jesus, but coming to believe does depend on personal encounter. Authentic encounter between persons only happens through mutual self-giving: Jesus' self-giving is shown through his gift of the Holy Spirit to us; our self-giving is shown when we open ourselves to receive that Spirit. Coming to believe more deeply that Jesus is risen and alive is the work of the Spirit within and among us. What a Gift!

Connecting the Responsorial Psalm to the Readings

In this Sunday's gospel the mercy of God is expressed in the sensitive manner in which Jesus responds to Thomas. Jesus accepts Thomas as he is—doubtful and uncertain—and gives him the physical proof he is demanding. Such is the love the risen Christ has for us that he comes to us when we are "hard pressed and . . . falling" (psalm) and turns our doubt, struggle, and fear into "strength and . . . courage" (psalm). As disciples of the Risen Christ, we also lead others from doubt to faith by our manner of relating to one another (first reading, gospel). We forgive one another, we share what we have, we gather for prayer, and we break the bread of the Eucharist. Our fidelity to Christian living makes the resurrection visible and leads the whole world to sing joyously that "[God's] mercy endures forever" (psalm).

Psalmist Preparation

In this Sunday's gospel Thomas seeks tangible proof that Jesus has risen from the dead. When the assembly looks at you leading the responsorial psalm do they see the presence of the risen Jesus? Do they see and hear in you his Spirit of self-giving?

Prayer

Redeeming God, may we lead others to belief in your Risen Son by being signs of your saving love to all whom we meet. We ask this through Christ our Lord. Amen.

Gospel (Luke 24:13-35; L46A)

That very day, the first day of the week, two of Jesus' disciples were going to a village seven miles from Jerusalem called Emmaus, and they were conversing about all the things that had occurred. And it happened that while they were conversing and debating, Jesus himself drew near and walked with them, but their eyes were prevented from recognizing him. He asked them, "What are you discussing as you walk along?" They stopped, looking downcast. One of them, named Cleopas, said to him in reply, "Are you the only visitor to Jerusalem who does not know of the things that have taken place there in these days?" And he replied to them, "What sort of things?" They said to him, "The things that happened to Jesus the Nazarene, who was a prophet mighty in deed and word before God and all the people, how our chief priests and rulers both handed him over to a sentence of death and crucified him. But we were hoping that he would be the one to redeem Israel; and besides all this, it is now the third day since this took place. Some women from our group, however, have astounded us: they were at the tomb early in the morning and did

not find his body; they came back and reported that they had indeed seen a vision of angels who announced that he was alive. Then some of those with us went to the tomb and found things just as the women had described, but him they did not see." And he said to them, "Oh, how foolish you are! How slow of heart to believe all that the prophets spoke! Was it not necessary that the Christ should suffer these things and enter into his glory?" Then beginning with Moses and all the prophets, he interpreted to them what referred to him in all the Scriptures. As they approached the village to which they were going, he gave the impression that he was going on farther. But they urged him, "Stay with us, for it is nearly evening and the day is almost over." So he went in to stay with them. And it happened that, while he was with them at table, he took bread, said the blessing, broke it, and gave it to them. With that their eyes were opened and they recognized him, but he vanished from their sight. Then they said to each other, "Were not our hearts burning within us while he spoke to us on the way and opened the Scriptures to us?" So they set out at once and returned to Jerusalem where they found gathered together the eleven and those with them who were saying, "The Lord has truly been raised and has appeared to Simon!" Then the two recounted what had taken place on the way and how he was made known to them in the breaking of bread.

First Reading (Acts 2:14, 22-33)
Then Peter stood up with the Eleven, raised his voice, and proclaimed: "You who are Jews, indeed all of you staying in Jerusalem. Let this be known to you, and listen to my words. You who are Israelites, hear these words. Jesus the Nazorean was a man commended to you by God with mighty deeds, wonders, and signs, which God worked through him in your midst, as you yourselves know. This man, delivered up by the set plan and foreknowledge of God, you killed, using lawless men to crucify him. But God raised him up, releasing him from the throes of death, because it was impossible for him to be held by it. For David says of him:

I saw the Lord ever before me,
with him at my right hand I shall not be disturbed.
Therefore my heart has been glad and my tongue has exulted;
my flesh, too, will dwell in hope,
because you will not abandon my soul to the netherworld,
nor will you suffer your holy one to see corruption.
You have made known to me the paths of life;
you will fill me with joy in your presence.

"My brothers, one can confidently say to you about the patriarch David that he died and was buried, and his tomb is in our midst to this day. But since he was a prophet and knew that God had sworn an oath to him that he would set one of his descendants upon his throne, he foresaw and spoke of the resurrection of the Christ, that neither was he abandoned to the netherworld nor did his flesh see corruption. God raised this Jesus; of this we are all witnesses. Exalted at the right hand of God, he received the promise of the Holy Spirit from the Father and poured him forth, as you see and hear."

Responsorial Psalm (Ps 16:1-2, 5, 7-8, 9-10, 11)

℟. (11a) Lord, you will show us the path of life. *or:* ℟. Alleluia.

Keep me, O God, for in you I take refuge;
    I say to the LORD, "My Lord are you."

O LORD, my allotted portion and my cup,
you it is who hold fast my lot.
℟. Lord, you will show us the path of life. *or:* ℟. Alleluia.

I bless the LORD who counsels me;
even in the night my heart exhorts me.
I set the LORD ever before me;
with him at my right hand I shall not be disturbed.
℟. Lord, you will show us the path of life. *or:* ℟. Alleluia.

Therefore my heart is glad and my soul rejoices,
my body, too, abides in confidence;
because you will not abandon my soul to the netherworld,
nor will you suffer your faithful one to undergo corruption.
℟. Lord, you will show us the path of life. *or:* ℟. Alleluia.

You will show me the path to life,
abounding joy in your presence,
the delights at your right hand forever.
℟. Lord, you will show us the path of life. *or:* ℟. Alleluia.

See Appendix, p. 216, for Second Reading

Reflecting on Living the Gospel

On our own we cannot grasp the mystery of the resurrection. The two disciples on the road to Emmaus were "conversing and debating"; they could recount the facts, but could not believe the mystery. Yet they greatly desired to move from disappointment and unbelief to hearts burning with Life and belief—they invited Jesus to stay the night with them. Our own participation in Word and sacrament must give rise to the same desire in us: to seek Life by journeying deeper into the mystery.

Connecting the Responsorial Psalm to the Readings

Psalm 16 is more than an argument Peter draws from the Old Testament to prove the resurrection (first reading). It is our profession of faith that the same life after death granted Jesus will be given to us. We, too, "[abide] in confidence" that God will not abandon our "[souls] to the netherworld" or our bodies to "corruption." The resurrection of Jesus is the foundation of our own hope (second reading).

Nonetheless, like the disciples on the road to Emmaus we struggle with doubts and misunderstandings about the mystery of the resurrection (gospel). The gospel shows us the many ways Christ comes to keep us walking along the "path to life"—in prayer and conversation, in reflection on Scripture, in the breaking of the bread. In Psalm 16 we proclaim these are not chance encounters but the concrete and constant ways God leads us along the "path of life."

Psalmist Preparation

In this responsorial psalm you acknowledge that God shows you the "path of life." The gospel reveals that this path is one of personal encounter with Christ who leads you through Scripture, Eucharist, and prayerful conversation to faith in his resurrection. When and how do you encounter Christ in these ways? Who helps you see and hear him? How in singing this psalm can you help the assembly see and hear him?

Prayer

Loving God, we thank you for sending your Son Jesus to show us the path to life and to accompany us along the way. Keep us faithful as we walk with him along the journey through death to fullness of life. We ask this through Christ our Lord. Amen.

Gospel (John 10:1-10; L49A)

Jesus said: "Amen, amen, I say to you, whoever does not enter a sheepfold through the gate but climbs over elsewhere is a thief and a robber. But whoever enters through the gate is the shepherd of the sheep. The gatekeeper opens it for him, and the sheep hear his voice, as the shepherd calls his own sheep by name and leads them out. When he has driven out all his own, he walks ahead of them, and the sheep follow him, because they recognize his voice. But they will not follow a stranger; they will run away from him, because they do not recognize the voice of strangers." Although Jesus used this figure of speech, the Pharisees did not realize what he was trying to tell them.

So Jesus said again, "Amen, amen, I say to you, I am the gate for the sheep. All who came before me are thieves and robbers, but the sheep did not listen to them. I am the gate. Whoever enters through me will be saved, and will come in and go out and find pasture. A thief comes only to steal and slaughter and destroy; I came so that they might have life and have it more abundantly."

First Reading (Acts 2:14a, 36-41)

Then Peter stood up with the Eleven, raised his voice, and proclaimed: "Let the whole house of Israel know for certain that God has made both Lord and Christ, this Jesus whom you crucified."

Now when they heard this, they were cut to the heart, and they asked Peter and the other apostles, "What are we to do, my brothers?" Peter said to them, "Repent and be baptized, every one of you, in the name of Jesus Christ for the forgiveness of your sins; and you will receive the gift of the Holy Spirit. For the promise is made to you and to your children and to all those far off, whomever the Lord our God will call." He testified with many other arguments, and was exhorting them, "Save yourselves from this corrupt generation." Those who accepted his message were baptized, and about three thousand persons were added that day.

Responsorial Psalm (Ps 23:1-3a, 3b-4, 5, 6)

℟. (1) The Lord is my shepherd; there is nothing I shall want.
or: ℟. Alleluia.

The LORD is my shepherd; I shall not want.
In verdant pastures he gives me repose;
beside restful waters he leads me;
    he refreshes my soul.

℟. The Lord is my shepherd; there is nothing I shall want.
or: ℟. Alleluia.

He guides me in right paths
    for his name's sake.
Even though I walk in the dark valley
    I fear no evil; for you are at my side
with your rod and your staff
    that give me courage.

℟. The Lord is my shepherd; there is nothing I shall want.
or: ℟. Alleluia.

You spread the table before me
    in the sight of my foes;
you anoint my head with oil;
    my cup overflows.

℟. The Lord is my shepherd; there is nothing I shall want.
or: ℟. Alleluia.

Only goodness and kindness follow me
    all the days of my life;
and I shall dwell in the house of the LORD
    for years to come.

℟. The Lord is my shepherd; there is nothing I shall want.
or: ℟. Alleluia.

See Appendix, p. 216, for Second Reading

Reflecting on Living the Gospel

Jesus states clearly that he came so that his followers might have abundant Life. Jesus uses the metaphor of a caring shepherd and sheep to indicate how his followers might receive that Life: by hearing his voice and their name, by following the Good Shepherd, by recognizing whose voice calls them. Hearing, following, recognizing: we are to open our ears in faith, open our hearts in trust, open our minds in love. This is the way to abundant Life. The Gate is wide open. Will we enter?

Connecting the Responsorial Psalm to the Readings
The readings this Sunday present us with two different examples of persons who have "gone astray like sheep" (second reading). In the first reading it is the people; in the gospel it is their leaders. The readings also present us with two very different responses to an encounter with the truth. Those listening to Peter are "cut to the heart" when they recognize what they have done. They immediately repent and are baptized. The Pharisees, on the other hand, refuse to acknowledge their destructive behavior, and in so doing remain cut off from Christ (gospel).

In the gospel Christ proclaims that he is both the shepherd and the gate into the sheepfold. He not only protects us from being led astray but also becomes the entryway of our return when we do stray. Peter's listeners grasp this, but the Pharisees remain obdurate in their unhearing. Our journey of discipleship will not be free of struggle or sidetracks (second reading), but the psalm assures us the One who is shepherd and gate will keep calling, keep guiding, keep leading us through the doorway to fullness of life. We have only to hear his voice and follow.

Psalmist Preparation
Psalm 23 promises Christ's loving and protective presence as you continue on your journey of discipleship. This journey is a long one and the possibilities of becoming lost, losing hope, being misled are real. But there is a Shepherd who is both by your side and up ahead of you, one who has already journeyed the way of death and resurrection and knows its path. As you sing, take his hand, and walk confidently.

Prayer
Gracious God, you sent your Son to shepherd us along the path to life. Help us always to hear and heed his voice and walk in the direction he points. We ask this through Christ our Lord. Amen.

Gospel (John 14:1-12; L52A)

Jesus said to his disciples: "Do not let your hearts be troubled. You have faith in God; have faith also in me. In my Father's house there are many dwelling places. If there were not, would I have told you that I am going to prepare a place for you? And if I go and prepare a place for you, I will come back again and take you to myself, so that where I am you also may be. Where I am going you know the way." Thomas said to him, "Master, we do not know where you are going; how can we know the way?" Jesus said to him, "I am the way and the truth and the life. No one

comes to the Father except through me. If you know me, then you will also know my Father. From now on you do know him and have seen him." Philip said to him, "Master, show us the Father, and that will be enough for us." Jesus said to him, "Have I been with you for so long a time and you still do not know me, Philip? Whoever has seen me has seen the Father. How can you say, 'Show us the Father'? Do you not believe that I am in the Father and the Father is in me? The words that I speak to you I do not speak on my own. The Father who dwells in me is doing his works. Believe me

that I am in the Father and the Father is in me, or else, believe because of the works themselves. Amen, amen, I say to you, whoever believes in me will do the works that I do, and will do greater ones than these, because I am going to the Father."

First Reading (Acts 6:1-7)

As the number of disciples continued to grow, the Hellenists complained against the Hebrews because their widows were being neglected in the daily distribution. So the Twelve called together the community of the disciples and said, "It is not right for us to neglect the word of God to serve at table. Brothers, select from among you seven reputable men, filled with the Spirit and wisdom, whom we shall appoint to this task, whereas we shall devote ourselves to prayer and to the ministry of the word." The proposal was acceptable to the whole community, so they chose Stephen, a man filled with faith and the Holy Spirit, also Philip, Prochorus, Nicanor, Timon, Parmenas, and Nicholas of Antioch, a convert to Judaism. They presented these men to the apostles who prayed and laid hands on them. The word of God continued to spread, and the number of the disciples in Jerusalem increased greatly; even a large group of priests were becoming obedient to the faith.

Responsorial Psalm (Ps 33:1-2, 4-5, 18-19)

℞. (22) Lord, let your mercy be on us, as we place our trust in you.
or: ℞. Alleluia.

Exult, you just, in the LORD;
 praise from the upright is fitting.
Give thanks to the LORD on the harp;
 with the ten-stringed lyre chant his praises.

℞. Lord, let your mercy be on us, as we place our trust in you.
or: ℞. Alleluia.

Upright is the word of the LORD,
 and all his works are trustworthy.
He loves justice and right;
 of the kindness of the LORD the earth is full.

℞. Lord, let your mercy be on us, as we place our trust in you.
or: ℞. Alleluia.

See, the eyes of the LORD are upon those who fear him,
 upon those who hope for his kindness,
to deliver them from death
 and preserve them in spite of famine.

℞. Lord, let your mercy be on us, as we place our trust in you.
or: ℞. Alleluia.

See Appendix, p. 217, for Second Reading

Reflecting on Living the Gospel

Jesus' words in this gospel from the Last Supper discourse are reassuring ones: "Do not let your hearts be troubled." The leap from the Jesus at the Last Supper to the Jesus after the resurrection is one giant step, one the disciples have not yet taken. But *we* have taken this leap. We are an Easter people. We have received the Holy Spirit who empowers us to know Jesus, through him to know the Father, and to do the works of Jesus. Believing this mitigates all troubles, all anxiety.

Connecting the Responsorial Psalm to the Readings

This Sunday's gospel depicts the disciples still mystified about Jesus even after years of intimate interaction with him. The first reading reveals the early church experiencing animosities among themselves. And the second reading indicates that faith in Christ is a choice some will make and others will not. The way of faith, then, is not so straightforward.

In the midst of these strifes and struggles, the psalm reminds us to trust in God whose word and works stand eternally trustworthy. And the gospel invites us to trust in Jesus who will show us the way we are to live. We needn't be troubled at Jesus' absence, then, for we have all the guidance we need. We are a chosen, holy, priestly people (second reading) who know the way we are to go (gospel) and have the capability to walk it. We have only to trust in God (psalm refrain) and to follow Jesus (gospel).

Psalmist Preparation

These verses from Psalm 33 convey utmost trust in God whose word is true, whose works are reliable, and whose kindness is granted to all who hope. In the gospel Jesus invites you to place this trust in him, for whoever knows him knows God. How has your celebration of this Easter season helped you grow in your knowledge of Jesus? What struggles with faith in him do you still experience? Who/what helps you to trust in him even in the midst of these struggles?

Prayer

Gracious God, you reveal yourself through your Son Jesus who speaks your words and shows us your works. May we come through him to

know who you are and to trust more fully in your promise of salvation. We ask this through Christ our Lord. Amen.

Gospel (John 14:15-21; L55A)

Jesus said to his disciples: "If you love me, you will keep my commandments. And I will ask the Father, and he will give you another Advocate to be with you always, the Spirit of truth, whom the world cannot accept, because it neither sees nor knows him. But you know him, because he remains with you, and will be in you. I will not leave you orphans; I will come to you. In a little while the world will no longer see me, but you will see me, because I live and you will live.

On that day you will realize that I am in my Father and you are in me and I in you. Whoever has my commandments and observes them is the one who loves me. And whoever loves me will be loved by my Father, and I will love him and reveal myself to him."

First Reading (Acts 8:5-8, 14-17)

Philip went down to the city of Samaria and proclaimed the Christ to them. With one accord, the crowds paid attention to what was said by Philip when they heard it and saw the signs he was doing. For unclean spirits, crying out in a loud voice, came out of many possessed people, and many paralyzed or crippled people were cured. There was great joy in that city.

Now when the apostles in Jerusalem heard that Samaria had accepted the word of God, they sent them Peter and John, who went down and prayed for them, that they might receive the Holy Spirit, for it had not yet fallen upon any of them; they had only been baptized in the name of the Lord Jesus. Then they laid hands on them and they received the Holy Spirit.

Responsorial Psalm (Ps 66:1-3, 4-5, 6-7, 16, 20)

℟. (1) Let all the earth cry out to God with joy. *or:* ℟. Alleluia.

Shout joyfully to God, all the earth,
    sing praise to the glory of his name;
    proclaim his glorious praise.
Say to God, "How tremendous are your deeds!"

℟. Let all the earth cry out to God with joy. *or:* ℟. Alleluia.

"Let all on earth worship and sing praise to you,
   sing praise to your name!"
Come and see the works of God,
   his tremendous deeds among the children of Adam.

℞. Let all the earth cry out to God with joy. *or:* ℞. Alleluia.

He has changed the sea into dry land;
   through the river they passed on foot.
Therefore let us rejoice in him.
   He rules by his might forever.

℞. Let all the earth cry out to God with joy. *or:* ℞. Alleluia.

Hear now, all you who fear God, while I declare
   what he has done for me.
Blessed be God who refused me not
   my prayer or his kindness!

℞. Let all the earth cry out to God with joy. *or:* ℞. Alleluia.

See Appendix, p. 217, for Second Reading

Reflecting on Living the Gospel

In John's gospel, "world" refers to everything opposed to God and being obedient to Jesus' commandments. The world sees neither Jesus nor the "Spirit of truth"; faithful disciples do. The world does not love; faithful disciples do. The world does not have life; faithful disciples do. Faithful disciples see, love, and live because of the Father's gift of the Spirit dwelling within them. This divine indwelling *is* God's very love. We are to be God's love made visible, that the world may see Jesus, come to the truth, and choose to live in faithful love.

Connecting the Responsorial Psalm to the Readings

In the verses of this responsorial psalm we "shout joyfully" about the culmination of God's "tremendous deeds" among us: the death and resurrection of Jesus. We also acclaim the "tremendous deed" of the gift of the Spirit poured into our hearts and flowing out into our actions (gospel, first reading). We have a great deal to sing about.

   The readings remind us, however, that we are to do more than sing about God's redemptive acts. We are to witness to them with conviction and power (first reading) and with "gentleness and reverence" (second reading). We are to do good because of them, even if this brings us suffering (second reading). Above all we are to reveal what God has wrought for humankind by keeping Jesus' commandments (gospel). Just as God's saving actions are the cause of our joyful singing, may our actions be cause for the whole world to sing.

Psalmist Preparation

This responsorial psalm reminds you that singing God's praises for the gift of redemption is not a private activity but a public proclamation. You invite "all on earth" to "hear" what you have to declare, to "come and see" what God has done, to join you in "glorious praise" of God. Your ministry as cantor, then, reaches far beyond the ears of the assembly gathered before you. Its dimensions are cosmic. As part of your preparation this week you might take some time to reflect on the awesome reach of your role and ask the Spirit to give you the grace to fulfill it.

Prayer

Redeeming God, by raising Jesus from death you bring us to new Life. We praise you for this great and marvelous deed. May we proclaim this tremendous deed to all the world both in the words we speak and in the way we live. We ask this through Christ our Lord. Amen.

Gospel (Matt 28:16-20; L58A)

The eleven disciples went to Galilee, to the mountain to which Jesus had ordered them. When they saw him, they worshiped, but they doubted. Then Jesus approached and said to them, "All power in heaven and on earth has been given to me. Go, therefore, and make disciples of all nations, baptizing them in the name of the Father, and of the Son, and of the Holy Spirit, teaching them to observe all that I have commanded you. And behold, I am with you always, until the end of the age."

First Reading (Acts 1:1-11)

In the first book, Theophilus, I dealt with all that Jesus did and taught until the day he was taken up, after giving instructions through the Holy Spirit to the apostles whom he had chosen. He presented himself alive to them by many proofs after he had suffered, appearing to them during forty days and speaking about the kingdom of God. While meeting with them, he enjoined them not to depart from Jerusalem, but to wait for "the promise of the Father about which you have heard me speak; for John baptized with water, but in a few days you will be baptized with the Holy Spirit."

When they had gathered together they asked him, "Lord, are you at this time going to restore the kingdom to Israel?" He answered them, "It is not for you to know the times or seasons that the Father has established by his own authority. But you will receive power when the Holy Spirit comes upon you, and you will be my witnesses in Jerusalem, throughout Judea and Samaria, and to the ends of the earth." When he had said this, as they were looking on, he was lifted up, and a cloud took him from their sight. While they were looking intently at the sky as he was going, suddenly two men dressed in white garments stood beside them. They said, "Men of Galilee, why are you standing there looking at the sky? This Jesus who has been taken up from you into heaven will return in the same way as you have seen him going into heaven."

Responsorial Psalm **(Ps 47:2-3, 6-7, 8-9)**

℞. (6) God mounts his throne to shouts of joy: a blare of trumpets for the
Lord. *or:* ℞. Alleluia.

All you peoples, clap your hands,
    shout to God with cries of gladness,
for the LORD, the Most High, the awesome,
    is the great king over all the earth.

℞. God mounts his throne to shouts of joy: a blare of trumpets for the
Lord. *or:* ℞. Alleluia.

God mounts his throne amid shouts of joy;
    the LORD, amid trumpet blasts.
Sing praise to God, sing praise;
    sing praise to our king, sing praise.

℞. God mounts his throne to shouts of joy: a blare of trumpets for the
Lord. *or:* ℞. Alleluia.

For king of all the earth is God;
    sing hymns of praise.
God reigns over the nations,
    God sits upon his holy throne.

℞. God mounts his throne to shouts of joy: a blare of trumpets for the
Lord. *or:* ℞. Alleluia.

See Appendix, p. 217, for Second Reading

Reflecting on Living the Gospel
The continuation of the mission is so important that Jesus issues the
most serious and unequivocal of directives. The disciples are to begin
where Jesus did, doing what Jesus did, but without geographical or tem-
poral limits: their mission is to "all nations" and continues "until the end
of the age." Jesus commissions not only those first disciples, but all those
through the ages who come to know and believe in him. Jesus chooses to
complete his work of salvation through us. We must choose to take up
his Great Commission.

Connecting the Responsorial Psalm to the Readings

Psalm 47 was an enthronement psalm used when the ark of the covenant was carried in procession into the temple. The Israelites clapped and shouted as they celebrated God's ascendancy over all heaven and earth. We use this psalm this day to acclaim that Christ has been given "all power in heaven and earth" (gospel). We sing it confident that Christ reigns even though we do not know the "time" when his kingdom will be fully manifest (first reading). We sing it even when the kingdom's delay generates doubts within us (gospel) for we "know what is the hope" to which we are called (second reading). We sing it even though Christ has disappeared from our midst because we know he nonetheless remains with us (gospel) and that his power flows through us (first reading). We sing it because we know Christ has won the victory over sin and death and nothing can prevail against him.

Psalmist Preparation

Psalm 47 presents a unique challenge for you. It is used for ascension in all three Lectionary years, and can easily be interpreted as referring only to this historical event in Christ's life. Your task is to move beyond historicizing to see how this psalm celebrates your and the assembly's participation in the mystery of Christ and his kingdom. As you prepare, ask the Spirit what this psalm has to do with you.

Prayer

God of glory, you raised us with your Son to be seated at your right hand. With him, we are victors over sin and death. With him, we sing your praises forever. Lead us, with him, to give our lives that all peoples may know the dignity to which you have called them. We ask this through Christ our Lord. Amen.

Gospel (John 17:1-11a; L59A)

Jesus raised his eyes to heaven and said, "Father, the hour has come. Give glory to your son, so that your son may glorify you, just as you gave him authority over all people, so that your son may give eternal life to all you gave him. Now this is eternal life, that they should know you, the only true God, and the one whom you sent, Jesus Christ. I glorified you on earth by accomplishing the work that you gave me to do. Now glorify me, Father, with you, with the glory that I had with you before the world began.

"I revealed your name to those whom you gave me out of the world. They belonged to you, and you gave them to me, and they have kept your word. Now they know that everything you gave me is from you, because the words you gave to me I have given to them, and they accepted them and truly understood that I came from you, and they have believed that you sent me. I pray for them. I do not pray for the world but for the ones you have given me, because they are yours, and everything of mine is yours and everything of yours is mine, and I have been glorified in them. And now I will no longer be in the world, but they are in the world, while I am coming to you."

First Reading (Acts 1:12-14)

After Jesus had been taken up to heaven the apostles returned to Jerusalem from the mount called Olivet, which is near Jerusalem, a sabbath day's journey away.

When they entered the city they went to the upper room where they were staying, Peter and John and James and Andrew, Philip and Thomas, Bartholomew and Matthew, James son of Alphaeus, Simon the Zealot, and Judas son of James. All these devoted themselves with one accord to prayer, together with some women, and Mary the mother of Jesus, and his brothers.

Responsorial Psalm (Ps 27:1, 4, 7-8)

R̸. (13) I believe that I shall see the good things of the Lord in the land of the living. *or:* R̸. Alleluia.

The LORD is my light and my salvation;
    whom should I fear?
The LORD is my life's refuge;
    of whom should I be afraid?

R̸. I believe that I shall see the good things of the Lord in the land of the living. *or:* R̸. Alleluia.

One thing I ask of the LORD; this I seek:
To dwell in the house of the LORD
    all the days of my life,
that I may gaze on the loveliness of the LORD
    and contemplate his temple.

R̸. I believe that I shall see the good things of the Lord in the land of the living. *or:* R̸. Alleluia.

Hear, O LORD, the sound of my call;
    have pity on me, and answer me.
Of you my heart speaks; you my glance seeks.

R̸. I believe that I shall see the good things of the Lord in the land of the living. *or:* R̸. Alleluia.

See Appendix, p. 218, for Second Reading

Reflecting on Living the Gospel

Jesus speaks of his and his Father's glory—but his words are not a reminiscing at the Last Supper of what has been but will soon be no more. No, this glory of which Jesus speaks is an eternal glory. Glory is the tangible trace in our world of God's holiness—who God is. Jesus' prayer is about his union with his Father, and it also expresses his desire for us to share in this same union, same glory, same holiness. Nothing of Jesus is withheld from us—he yearns to give us eternal Life.

Connecting the Responsorial Psalm to the Readings

After Jesus' ascension the disciples find themselves in an in-between time of waiting for the descent of the Spirit. They immerse themselves in prayer (first reading). We, too, live in an in-between time, waiting not for the coming of the Spirit but for the return of Christ in glory and for the full flowering of his kingdom. The second reading warns that if we remain faithful to Christ during this time of waiting we will be made to suffer for it. Because he is fully aware of what our waiting and our fidelity will entail, Jesus prays for us (gospel).

The responsorial psalm captures the content of our prayer in response. We tell Christ that we believe in the "good things" he has promised. We tell Christ that we fear nothing, for in this time of long darkness he is our "light and our salvation." We tell Christ that we desire only one thing, to dwell with him and to know him more intimately. And we beg him to have compassion for us. For we know, as he does, the costs to discipleship and the dangers to faith that this long wait holds. May our prayer remain ever joined with his.

Psalmist Preparation

The confidence in God the responsorial psalm expresses is couched in intimations of danger: "whom should I fear?" and "Hear, O Lord, the sound of my call." As the second reading indicates the glory to be yours because of faithful discipleship will come only because you have first suffered for Christ. When you sing this psalm, then, you are acknowledging the real challenge of discipleship and asking for God's help in meeting it. When you reflect on this challenge what makes you afraid? How does Christ help you with this fear?

Prayer

Faithful God, as we await the return of Christ in glory keep us free from fear and steady in discipleship. Guide our gaze to look only upon the good things you have in store for us. We ask this through Christ our Lord. Amen.

Gospel (John 20:19-23; L63A)
On the evening of that first day of the week, when the doors were locked, where the disciples were, for fear of the Jews, Jesus came and stood in their midst and said to them, "Peace be with you." When he had said this, he showed them his hands and his side. The disciples rejoiced when they saw the Lord. Jesus said to them again, "Peace be with you. As the Father has sent me, so I send you." And when he had said this, he breathed on them and said to them, "Receive the Holy Spirit. Whose sins you forgive are forgiven them, and whose sins you retain are retained."

First Reading (Acts 2:1-11)
When the time for Pentecost was fulfilled, they were all in one place together. And suddenly there came from the sky a noise like a strong driving wind, and it filled the entire house in which they were. Then there appeared to them tongues as of fire, which parted and came to rest on each one of them. And they were all filled with the Holy Spirit and began to speak in different tongues, as the Spirit enabled them to proclaim.

Now there were devout Jews from every nation under heaven staying in Jerusalem. At this sound, they gathered in a large crowd, but they were confused because each one heard them speaking in his own language. They were astounded, and in amazement they asked, "Are not all these people who are speaking Galileans? Then how does each of us hear them in his native language? We are Parthians, Medes, and Elamites, inhabitants of Mesopotamia, Judea and Cappadocia, Pontus and Asia, Phrygia and Pamphylia, Egypt and the districts of Libya near Cyrene, as well as travelers from Rome, both Jews and converts to Judaism, Cretans and Arabs, yet we hear them speaking in our own tongues of the mighty acts of God."

Responsorial Psalm (Ps 104:1, 24, 29-30, 31, 34)

℟. (cf. 30) Lord, send out your Spirit, and renew the face of the earth.
or: ℟. Alleluia.

Bless the LORD, O my soul!
O LORD, my God, you are great indeed!
How manifold are your works, O LORD!
The earth is full of your creatures.

℟. Lord, send out your Spirit, and renew the face of the earth.
or: ℟. Alleluia.

If you take away their breath, they perish
and return to their dust.
When you send forth your spirit, they are created,
and you renew the face of the earth.

℟. Lord, send out your Spirit, and renew the face of the earth.
or: ℟. Alleluia.

May the glory of the LORD endure forever;
may the LORD be glad in his works!
Pleasing to him be my theme;
I will be glad in the LORD.

℟. Lord, send out your Spirit, and renew the face of the earth.
or: ℟. Alleluia.

See Appendix, p. 218, for Second Reading

Reflecting on Living the Gospel

One of the fruits of the Holy Spirit is peace. This peace is not a passive state of tranquility, but an empowering force which allays our fears, urges us forth to take up Jesus' mission, and instills in us forgiving hearts. This peace transforms how we see ourselves, how we pursue discipleship, and how we relate to the world and one another. Certainly, this peace is life-encompassing and enduring. How much more so is Jesus' gift of the Holy Spirit!

Connecting the Responsorial Psalm to the Readings

Psalm 104 is deliberately patterned after the story of creation as recounted in Genesis 1. The psalm unfolds in seven sections dealing with different aspects of God's mighty creative acts. In the verses which we use for Pentecost we proclaim that God's works are manifold. We pray that God be "glad in [these] works." The good news is that the "mighty acts of God" (first reading) will endure because we have been empowered to continue them (gospel). Jesus has breathed upon us his very Spirit and sent us to carry out the Spirit's greatest work: the granting of peace through forgiveness of sins. The work of the Spirit is the constant renewal of relationship between us and God, us and one another, us and the whole of the created world. Truly God is glad in this work and glad in us who do it.

Psalmist Preparation

When you sing this psalm refrain you pray that God send the Spirit upon you, that the renewal of the earth occur in and through you. This is a big commission. Are you willing to take it on?

Prayer

Creating God, you continually send your Spirit to renew our relationships through the power of forgiveness. Open our hearts to hear what the Spirit teaches and strengthen our wills to do as the Spirit directs that the face of the earth may be renewed. We ask this through Christ our Lord. Amen.

JUNE 15, 2014

Gospel (John 3:16-18; L164A)

God so loved the world that he gave his only Son, so that everyone who believes in him might not perish but might have eternal life. For God did not send his Son into the world to condemn the world, but that the world might be saved through him. Whoever believes in him will not be condemned, but whoever does not believe has already been condemned, because he has not believed in the name of the only Son of God.

First Reading (Exod 34:4b-6, 8-9)

Early in the morning Moses went up Mount Sinai as the LORD had commanded him, taking along the two stone tablets.

Having come down in a cloud, the LORD stood with Moses there and proclaimed his name, "LORD." Thus the LORD passed before him and cried out, "The LORD, the LORD, a merciful and gracious God, slow to anger and rich in kindness and fidelity." Moses at once bowed down to the ground in worship. Then he said, "If I find favor with you, O LORD, do come along in our company. This is indeed a stiff-necked people; yet pardon our wickedness and sins, and receive us as your own."

Responsorial Psalm (Dan 3:52, 53, 54, 55)

R̸. (52b) Glory and praise forever!

Blessed are you, O Lord, the God of our fathers,
    praiseworthy and exalted above all forever;
and blessed is your holy and glorious name,
    praiseworthy and exalted above all for all ages.

R̸. Glory and praise forever!

Blessed are you in the temple of your holy glory,
    praiseworthy and glorious above all forever.

R̸. Glory and praise forever!

Blessed are you on the throne of your kingdom,
    praiseworthy and exalted above all forever.

R̸. Glory and praise forever!

Blessed are you who look into the depths
  from your throne upon the cherubim,
  praiseworthy and exalted above all forever.
℟. Glory and praise forever!

See Appendix, p. 218, for Second Reading

Reflecting on Living the Gospel
God's desire is that we share in divine Life eternally. To this end, God is very near—near to Moses on Mount Sinai and near to us in the divine Son who came to dwell among us. Even more: for those who believe, our triune God dwells *within* us by grace and communion, drawing us into the inner Life of the Trinity. The unceasing Life of the Trinity is this: to love us into eternal Life. It is God's gracious gift, and ours to choose.

Connecting the Responsorial Psalm to the Readings
Daniel 3:52-56 is an addition (included in Roman Catholic but not Jewish or Protestant versions of the Old Testament) to the story of the three men thrown into the fiery furnace because they would not worship the Babylonian gods. The verses are part of a lengthy song of praise sung by the men as they moved about in the furnace, untouched by the flames. When King Nebuchadnezzar peered inside he was amazed to see that they were alive and unharmed, and that a fourth "person" walked among them. He immediately released them and declared their God mighty above all others.

The first and second readings tell us this mighty God is merciful, gracious, slow to anger, kind, faithful, full of love and peace. The gospel tells us something even more amazing: this God gives "his only Son" that we might have fullness of Life. What makes our God mighty is an unlimited capacity for self-giving love. And we are the recipients of this love! No wonder we want to shout, "Blessed are you . . . Glory and praise forever!" (psalm)

Psalmist Preparation
An excellent preparation for leading this canticle would be to use part of it (e.g., Blessed are you, God! or, Glory and praise to you, God!) as a personal prayer every day this week. Sing it as you rise each morning, as you see new spring life pushing up from the ground, as you look upon the face of a loved one, as you share a meal. Sing it wherever you see

pain eased, forgiveness given, hope rekindled. You will be celebrating the God in whom you believe and the assembly will hear this in your singing on Sunday.

Prayer

Almighty Triune God, you bless us with mercy, kindness, love, and peace. Above all, you bless us with the gift of Jesus sent to free us from sin and death. May we live always in your love, may we act always as temples of your presence. We ask this through Christ our Lord. Amen.

Gospel (John 6:51-58; L167A)

Jesus said to the Jewish crowds: "I am the living bread that came down from heaven; whoever eats this bread will live forever; and the bread that I will give is my flesh for the life of the world."

The Jews quarreled among themselves, saying, "How can this man give us his flesh to eat?" Jesus said to them, "Amen, amen, I say to you, unless you eat the flesh of the Son of Man and drink his blood, you do not have life within you. Whoever eats my flesh and drinks my blood has eternal life, and I will raise him on the last day. For my flesh is true food, and my blood is true drink. Whoever eats my flesh and drinks my blood remains in me and I in him. Just as the living Father sent me and I have life because of the Father, so also the one who feeds on me will have life because of me. This is the bread that came down from heaven. Unlike your ancestors who ate and still died, whoever eats this bread will live forever."

First Reading (Deut 8:2-3, 14b-16a)

Moses said to the people: "Remember how for forty years now the LORD, your God, has directed all your journeying in the desert, so as to test you by affliction and find out whether or not it was your intention to keep his commandments. He therefore let you be afflicted with hunger, and then fed you with manna, a food unknown to you and your fathers, in order to show you that not by bread alone does one live, but by every word that comes forth from the mouth of the LORD.

"Do not forget the LORD, your God, who brought you out of the land of Egypt, that place of slavery; who guided you through the vast and terrible desert with its saraph serpents and scorpions, its parched and waterless ground; who brought forth water for you from the flinty rock and fed you in the desert with manna, a food unknown to your fathers."

Responsorial Psalm **(Ps 147:12-13, 14-15, 19-20)**

℟. (12) Praise the Lord, Jerusalem. *or:* ℟. Alleluia.

Glorify the LORD, O Jerusalem;
    praise your God, O Zion.
For he has strengthened the bars of your gates;
    he has blessed your children within you.

℟. Praise the Lord, Jerusalem. *or:* ℟. Alleluia.

He has granted peace in your borders;
    with the best of wheat he fills you.
He sends forth his command to the earth;
    swiftly runs his word!

℟. Praise the Lord, Jerusalem. *or:* ℟. Alleluia.

He has proclaimed his word to Jacob,
    his statutes and his ordinances to Israel.
He has not done thus for any other nation;
    his ordinances he has not made known to them. Alleluia.

℟. Praise the Lord, Jerusalem. *or:* ℟. Alleluia.

See Appendix, p. 218, for Second Reading

Reflecting on Living the Gospel

Jesus' declaration that he is the "bread that came down from heaven" grounds his further declaration that those who eat "this bread will live forever." Heaven is a state of forever; those who eat the One come down from heaven will be like he is—in a state of forever. This lofty promise is not a dream. It is real because Jesus himself has passed from this life to eternal glory. His humanity has risen and now lives forever. It is this risen humanity which is our nourishment for eternal Life.

Connecting the Responsorial Psalm to the Readings

In the first reading Moses admonishes the Israelites never to forget all that God has done for them. God has freed them from slavery, directed their steps through the desert, taught them patiently to obey the commands of the covenant, and, in the midst of great hunger, fed them with a "food unknown" to their ancestors.

In the gospel Jesus also offers a food previously unknown on earth, his very flesh and blood to eat and drink. Jesus' immediate hearers are stunned by his words and become divided and fractious (gospel). But we who believe in his words and choose to partake of his flesh become one with him and with each other (second reading). We participate in the very mystery of Christ and become his body. We eat the "best of wheat" (psalm) and are born into eternal Life.

Psalmist Preparation

God fills you "with the best of wheat" in the Eucharist, the very Body and Blood of Jesus. Take time this week to thank God for the gift of the Eucharist and for the union with Christ (gospel) and with all the members of the Body of Christ (second reading) the Eucharist brings. Then you will truly "Praise the Lord" with full heart when you sing this psalm.

Prayer

Nourishing God, in the gift of your Son you feed us with the best of wheat and fill us with abundant life. May our feasting on his Body and Blood strengthen us to hand over our bodies as nourishment of others. We ask this through Christ our Lord. Amen.

Gospel (Matt 16:13-19; L591)

When Jesus went into the region of Caesarea Philippi
   he asked his disciples,
   "Who do people say that the Son of Man is?"
They replied, "Some say John the Baptist, others Elijah,
   still others Jeremiah or one of the
      prophets."
He said to them, "But who do you say that I
   am?"
Simon Peter said in reply,
   "You are the Christ, the Son of the living
   God."
Jesus said to him in reply, "Blessed are you,
   Simon son of Jonah.
For flesh and blood has not revealed this to
   you, but my heavenly Father.
And so I say to you, you are Peter,
   and upon this rock I will build my Church,
   and the gates of the netherworld shall not prevail against it.
I will give you the keys to the Kingdom of heaven.
Whatever you bind on earth shall be bound in heaven;
   and whatever you loose on earth shall be loosed in heaven."

First Reading (Acts 12:1-11)

In those days, King Herod laid hands upon some members of the Church
   to harm them.
He had James, the brother of John, killed by the sword,
   and when he saw that this was pleasing to the Jews
   he proceeded to arrest Peter also.
—It was the feast of Unleavened Bread.—
He had him taken into custody and put in prison
   under the guard of four squads of four soldiers each.
He intended to bring him before the people after Passover.
Peter thus was being kept in prison,
   but prayer by the Church was fervently being made
   to God on his behalf.

On the very night before Herod was to bring him to trial,
Peter, secured by double chains,
was sleeping between two soldiers,
while outside the door guards kept watch on the prison.
Suddenly the angel of the Lord stood by him,
and a light shone in the cell.
He tapped Peter on the side and awakened him, saying,
"Get up quickly."
The chains fell from his wrists.
The angel said to him, "Put on your belt and your sandals."
He did so.
Then he said to him, "Put on your cloak and follow me."
So he followed him out,
not realizing that what was happening through the angel was real;
he thought he was seeing a vision.
They passed the first guard, then the second,
and came to the iron gate leading out to the city,
which opened for them by itself.
They emerged and made their way down an alley,
and suddenly the angel left him.
Then Peter recovered his senses and said,
"Now I know for certain that the Lord sent his angel
and rescued me from the hand of Herod
and from all that the Jewish people had been expecting."

Responsorial Psalm (Ps 34:2-3, 4-5, 6-7, 8-9)

R7. (8) The angel of the Lord will rescue those who fear him.

I will bless the LORD at all times;
    his praise shall be ever in my mouth.
Let my soul glory in the LORD;
    the lowly will hear me and be glad.

R7. The angel of the Lord will rescue those who fear him.

Glorify the LORD with me,
    let us together extol his name.
I sought the LORD, and he answered me
    and delivered me from all my fears.

R7. The angel of the Lord will rescue those who fear him.

Look to him that you may be radiant with joy,
  and your faces may not blush with shame.
When the poor one called out, the LORD heard,
  and from all his distress he saved him.

R⁊. The angel of the Lord will rescue those who fear him.

The angel of the LORD encamps
  around those who fear him, and delivers them.
Taste and see how good the LORD is;
  blessed the man who takes refuge in him.

R⁊. The angel of the Lord will rescue those who fear him.

See Appendix, p. 218, for Second Reading

Reflecting on Living the Gospel

To be faithful rocks upon which the church is built, we must know who
Jesus is for us, listen to what he teaches us, and guard against anything
prevailing against his church. Peter and Paul's faithful and fruitful discipleship rested on the rock of their knowing Jesus; so must ours. Drawing
from our everyday experience of rocks, we must be unyielding when it
comes to living what Jesus has taught us, rock solid when it comes to following him, rock steady in our commitment to bring his love and care to
others.

Connecting the Responsorial Psalm to the Readings

The responsorial psalm verses for this solemnity are taken from Psalm
34. In grave danger, the psalmist called on God and was rescued. Now
the psalmist cannot hold herself or himself back from telling the lowly
what God has done. The psalmist promises that all who take refuge in
God will be protected in time of trouble.

Peter and Paul suffered persecution for proclaiming who Christ was
(first and second readings). What enabled them to remain faithful to their
mission was their rock solid trust in God's ultimate protection (second
reading and gospel). Our celebration of their lives reminds us of our call
to participate in their mission and to stand fast when that mission brings
us hardship, resistance, and suffering. In singing this psalm we proclaim
our steadfast faith in God's protection no matter what we face for our fidelity. We join in the faith of Peter and Paul, our foundational figures,
and build our lives on fidelity to our mission and confidence in God.

Psalmist Preparation

How is your ministry as a cantor a participation in the mission of the church? How does your ministry help others come to know who Christ is? Do you proclaim him, and only him, to the assembly when you sing?

Prayer

God of our salvation, you give us Saints Peter and Paul as models of courage, confidence, and fidelity. May we, like them, be courageous in proclaiming the Good News, confident of your constant protection, and faithful to all that Christ has taught. We ask this through Christ our Lord. Amen.

Gospel (Matt 11:25-30; L100A)

At that time Jesus exclaimed: "I give praise to you, Father, Lord of heaven and earth, for although you have hidden these things from the wise and the learned you have revealed them to little ones. Yes, Father, such has been your gracious will. All things have been handed over to me by my Father. No one knows the Son except the Father, and no one knows the Father except the Son and anyone to whom the Son wishes to reveal him.

"Come to me, all you who labor and are burdened, and I will give you rest. Take my yoke upon you and learn from me, for I am meek and humble of heart; and you will find rest for yourselves. For my yoke is easy, and my burden light."

First Reading (Zech 9:9-10)

Thus says the LORD:

Rejoice heartily, O daughter Zion,
shout for joy, O daughter Jerusalem!
See, your king shall come to you;
a just savior is he,
meek, and riding on an ass,
on a colt, the foal of an ass.
He shall banish the chariot from Ephraim,
and the horse from Jerusalem;
the warrior's bow shall be banished,
and he shall proclaim peace to the nations.
His dominion shall be from sea to sea,
and from the River to the ends of the earth.

Responsorial Psalm (Ps 145:1-2, 8-9, 10-11, 13-14)

R̸. (cf. 1) I will praise your name forever, my king and my God.
or: R̸. Alleluia.

I will extol you, O my God and King,
and I will bless your name forever and ever.
Every day will I bless you,
and I will praise your name forever and ever.

R̸. I will praise your name forever, my king and my God. *or:* R̸. Alleluia.

The LORD is gracious and merciful,
  slow to anger and of great kindness.
The LORD is good to all
  and compassionate toward all his works.

℟. I will praise your name forever, my king and my God. *or:* ℟. Alleluia.

Let all your works give you thanks, O LORD,
  and let your faithful ones bless you.
Let them discourse of the glory of your kingdom
  and speak of your might.

℟. I will praise your name forever, my king and my God. *or:* ℟. Alleluia.

The LORD is faithful in all his words
  and holy in all his works.
The LORD lifts up all who are falling
  and raises up all who are bowed down.

℟. I will praise your name forever, my king and my God. *or:* ℟. Alleluia.

Second Reading (Rom 8:9, 11-13)

Reflecting on Living the Gospel

What are the things hidden from the wise but revealed to little ones? The previous verses from Matthew's chapter 11 indicate that "these things" are the destruction resulting from being unfaithful to God's "gracious will." The "little ones" are those who, having received Jesus' revelation about the Father, remain faithful and enter into God's reign of peace. The faithful, having come to Jesus and taken his yoke upon themselves, live in God's peace now. These faithful ones need have no fear of Jesus' judgment.

Connecting the Responsorial Psalm to the Readings

In the gospel Jesus invites us to take up the yoke of revealing to the world what has been revealed to us: the mystery of who God is. This God comes humbly (first reading and gospel) to raise up those who are bowed down (psalm). The commission Jesus gives us, then, does not add burdens to the backs of people but lifts them. Nor does it add burdens to our own shoulders for the very work, Jesus promises, will bring us rest (gospel).

In a subtle way the responsorial psalm shows us how this promise is fulfilled. By alternating between shouting God's praises (strophes 1 and 3) and proclaiming God's nature (strophes 2 and 4), the psalm indicates that the very work of acknowledging God to the world leads to deeper knowledge of who God is. The very mission itself leads us closer to the God of mercy and compassion. Such work is, then, ultimately freeing and easeful. May we take it up with joy.

Psalmist Preparation
In a sense every time you sing a responsorial psalm you reveal some aspect of God and God's "gracious will" (gospel) to the assembly. How has this ministry led you yourself to know God more deeply? How has it offered you "rest" (gospel)?

Prayer
Good and kind God, you place upon our shoulders not heavy burdens but the yoke of Christ. May we joyously share his work of making you known to all the world. We ask this through Christ our Lord. Amen.

Gospel (Matt 13:1-23 [or shorter form Matt 13:1-9]; L103A)

On that day, Jesus went out of the house and sat down by the sea. Such large crowds gathered around him that he got into a boat and sat down, and the whole crowd stood along the shore. And he spoke to them at length in parables, saying: "A sower went out to sow. And as he sowed, some seed fell on the path, and birds came and ate it up. Some fell on rocky ground, where it had little soil. It sprang up at once because the soil was not deep, and when the sun rose it was scorched, and it withered for lack of roots. Some seed fell among thorns, and the thorns grew up and choked it. But some seed fell on rich soil, and produced fruit, a hundred or sixty or thirtyfold. Whoever has ears ought to hear."

The disciples approached him and said, "Why do you speak to them in parables?" He said to them in reply, "Because knowledge of the mysteries of the kingdom of heaven has been granted to you, but to them it has not been granted. To anyone who has, more will be given and he will grow rich; from anyone who has not, even what he has will be taken away. This is why I speak to them in parables, because

they look but do not see and hear but do not listen or understand.
Isaiah's prophecy is fulfilled in them, which says:
You shall indeed hear but not understand,
you shall indeed look but never see.
Gross is the heart of this people,
they will hardly hear with their ears,
they have closed their eyes,
lest they see with their eyes
and hear with their ears
and understand with their hearts and be converted,
and I heal them.

"But blessed are your eyes, because they see, and your ears, because they hear. Amen, I say to you, many prophets and righteous people longed to see what you see but did not see it, and to hear what you hear but did not hear it.

"Hear then the parable of the sower. The seed sown on the path is the one who hears the word of the kingdom without understanding it, and the evil one comes and steals away what was sown in his heart. The seed sown on rocky ground is the one who hears the word and receives it at once with joy. But he has no root and lasts only for a time. When some tribulation or persecution comes because of the word, he immediately falls away. The seed sown among thorns is the one who hears the word, but then worldly anxiety and the lure of riches choke the word and it bears no fruit. But the seed sown on rich soil is the one who hears the word and understands it, who indeed bears fruit and yields a hundred or sixty or thirtyfold."

First Reading (Isa 55:10-11)
Thus says the LORD:
Just as from the heavens
    the rain and snow come down
and do not return there
    till they have watered the earth,
    making it fertile and fruitful,
giving seed to the one who sows
    and bread to the one who eats,
so shall my word be
    that goes forth from my mouth;
my word shall not return to me void,
    but shall do my will,
    achieving the end for which I sent it.

Responsorial Psalm (Ps 65:10, 11, 12-13, 14)
R⁄. (Luke 8:8) The seed that falls on good ground will yield a fruitful harvest.

You have visited the land and watered it;
    greatly have you enriched it.
God's watercourses are filled;
    you have prepared the grain.
R⁄. The seed that falls on good ground will yield a fruitful harvest.

Thus have you prepared the land: drenching its furrows,
    breaking up its clods,
softening it with showers,
    blessing its yield.
R⁄. The seed that falls on good ground will yield a fruitful harvest.

You have crowned the year with your bounty,
    and your paths overflow with a rich harvest;
the untilled meadows overflow with it,
    and rejoicing clothes the hills.

℟. The seed that falls on good ground will yield a fruitful harvest.

The fields are garmented with flocks
    and the valleys blanketed with grain.
    They shout and sing for joy.

℟. The seed that falls on good ground will yield a fruitful harvest.

Second Reading (Rom 8:18-23)

Reflecting on Living the Gospel

Jesus explicitly connects the seed with "one who hears the word." Some hear but no growth happens. Others hear and the word is nurtured and produces good fruit. Both in the parable itself and in Jesus' explanation of it, he indicates that seeds falling on rich soil do not all produce the same abundance—some thirty, some sixty, some a hundredfold. God cares less about quantity produced and more about growth and life coming to fruition. God actually gives us more than even a hundredfold. God gives us fullness of Life forever.

Connecting the Responsorial Psalm to the Readings

The parable of the sower and the seed (gospel) indicates that some seed will not bear fruit, but the responsorial psalm promises that God will bring about abundant harvest no matter what the conditions of the planting. God not only plants, God prepares the soil by watering it, softening it, breaking up its clods—so much so that even untended meadows burst with harvest. Nothing will impede the will of God's word (first reading).

How wonderful that God persists in visiting the "land" of our hearts and working it until we yield to receiving what God desires to plant. How wonderful that the word of God is stronger than any resistance we or the world put up against it. No matter that we are slow to receive the seed, reticent to let it grow, distracted from the task, God will bring what has been planted to abundant harvest. Let us, with all the fields and valleys, shout and sing for joy!

Psalmist Preparation

Part of the good news of this responsorial psalm is that no ground, no matter how poor, is left untilled by God. God will tend to whatever dryness or clods are in the way of your receiving God's word, nurturing it and letting it grow. You have only to let God do this work. The "good ground" of the refrain, then, is not a judgment, but a promise. So sing with hope and with thanksgiving!

Prayer

God of fruitfulness, you sow the seed of your presence in our hearts. Make that seed grow to full harvest that all we meet may see your face. We ask this through Christ our Lord. Amen.

Gospel (Matt 13:24-43 [or shorter form Matt 13:24-30]; L106A)

Jesus proposed another parable to the crowds, saying: "The kingdom of heaven may be likened to a man who sowed good seed in his field. While everyone was asleep his enemy came and sowed weeds all through the wheat, and then went off. When the crop grew and bore fruit, the weeds appeared as well. The slaves of the householder came to him and said, 'Master, did you not sow good seed in your field? Where have the weeds come from?' He answered, 'An enemy has done this.' His slaves said to

him, 'Do you want us to go and pull them up?' He replied, 'No, if you pull up the weeds you might uproot the wheat along with them. Let them grow together until harvest; then at harvest time I will say to the harvesters, "First collect the weeds and tie them in bundles for burning; but gather the wheat into my barn."'"

He proposed another parable to them. "The kingdom of heaven is like a mustard seed that a person took and sowed in a field. It is the smallest of all the seeds, yet when full-grown it is the largest of plants. It becomes a large bush, and the 'birds of the sky come and dwell in its branches.'"

He spoke to them another parable. "The kingdom of heaven is like yeast that a woman took and mixed with three measures of wheat flour until the whole batch was leavened."

All these things Jesus spoke to the crowds in parables. He spoke to them only in parables, to fulfill what had been said through the prophet:

"I will open my mouth in parables,
I will announce what has lain hidden from the foundation of
the world."

Then, dismissing the crowds, he went into the house. His disciples approached him and said, "Explain to us the parable of the weeds in the field." He said in reply, "He who sows good seed is the Son of Man, the field is the world, the good seed the children of the kingdom. The weeds are the children of the evil one, and the enemy who sows them is the devil. The harvest is the end of the age, and the harvesters are angels. Just as weeds are collected and burned up with fire, so will it be at the end of the age. The Son of Man will send his angels, and they will collect out of his kingdom all who cause others to sin and all evildoers. They will throw them into the fiery furnace, where there will be wailing and grinding of teeth. Then the righteous will shine like the sun in the kingdom of their Father. Whoever has ears ought to hear."

First Reading (Wis 12:13, 16-19)

There is no god besides you who have the care of all,
   that you need show you have not unjustly condemned.
For your might is the source of justice;
   your mastery over all things makes you lenient to all.
For you show your might when the perfection of your power is
      disbelieved;
   and in those who know you, you rebuke temerity.
But though you are master of might, you judge with clemency,
   and with much lenience you govern us;
   for power, whenever you will, attends you.
And you taught your people, by these deeds,
   that those who are just must be kind;
and you gave your children good ground for hope
   that you would permit repentance for their sins.

Responsorial Psalm (Ps 86:5-6, 9-10, 15-16)

R̸. (5a) Lord, you are good and forgiving.

You, O Lord, are good and forgiving,
   abounding in kindness to all who call upon you.
Hearken, O Lord, to my prayer
   and attend to the sound of my pleading.

R̸. Lord, you are good and forgiving.

All the nations you have made shall come
   and worship you, O Lord,
   and glorify your name.
For you are great, and you do wondrous deeds;
   you alone are God.

R̸. Lord, you are good and forgiving.

You, O Lord, are a God merciful and gracious,
   slow to anger, abounding in kindness and fidelity.
Turn toward me, and have pity on me;
   give your strength to your servant.

R̸. Lord, you are good and forgiving.

Second Reading (Rom 8:26-27)

Reflecting on Living the Gospel

"The kingdom of heaven is like . . . " Jesus uses three comparisons to explain this mystery of God's Presence and reign. The first parable speaks of discernment; the second of full growth; the third of transformation. In this is the realization of the kingdom of heaven: our discerning God's will, our growing into full stature as "children of the kingdom," opening ourselves to being transformed into those remaining faithful until "the end of the age." The kingdom of heaven is at hand when we allow God to be present to us and we become that Presence for others.

Connecting the Responsorial Psalm to the Readings

In these verses from Psalm 86 we beg God to listen to our pleading and give us strength. The parables told by Jesus in the gospel make clear the cause of our begging: alongside the good God has planted in the church and the world, so much bad exists; so many starts toward the coming of the kingdom are just insignificant, tiny seeds; a little yeast leavens a measure of flour, but the work of kneading must first be done if the bread is to rise. We need the grace of patience and persistence. And we need the kindness of God, this God who understands how slow growth can be (gospel) and who leaves needed room for repentance (first reading). In singing this psalm we ask this "good and forgiving" God (psalm refrain) to give us a share in divine leniency, patience, and strength.

Psalmist Preparation

What gives you confidence that God is bringing the kingdom of heaven to full growth within you? within the world? When and where do you need God's patience, leniency, and kindness with yourself? with others?

Prayer

Patient God, you give us the time we need to grow to full stature as your sons and daughters. Help us to grant that same forbearance to one another. We ask this through Christ our Lord. Amen.

Gospel (Matt 13:44-52 [or shorter form Matt 13:44-46]; L109A)

Jesus said to his disciples: "The kingdom of heaven is like a treasure buried in a field, which a person finds and hides again, and out of joy goes and sells all that he has and buys that field. Again, the kingdom of heaven is like a merchant searching for fine pearls. When he finds a pearl of great price, he goes and sells all that he has and buys it. Again, the kingdom of heaven is like a net thrown into the sea, which collects fish of every kind. When it is full they haul it ashore and sit down to put what is good into buckets. What is bad they throw away. Thus it will be at the end of the age. The angels will go out and separate the wicked from the righteous and throw them into the fiery furnace, where there will be wailing and grinding of teeth.

"Do you understand all these things?" They answered, "Yes." And he replied, "Then every scribe who has been instructed in the kingdom of heaven is like the head of a household who brings from his storeroom both the new and the old."

First Reading (1 Kgs 3:5, 7-12)

The LORD appeared to Solomon in a dream at night. God said, "Ask something of me and I will give it to you." Solomon answered: "O LORD, my God, you have made me, your servant, king to succeed my father David; but I am a mere youth, not knowing at all how to act. I serve you in the midst of the people whom you have chosen, a people so vast that it cannot be numbered or counted. Give your servant, therefore, an understanding heart to judge your people and to distinguish right from wrong. For who is able to govern this vast people of yours?"

The LORD was pleased that Solomon made this request. So God said to him: "Because you have asked for this— not for a long life for yourself, nor for riches, nor for the life of your enemies, but for understanding so that you may know what is right— I do as you requested. I give you a heart so wise and understanding that there has never been anyone like you up to now, and after you there will come no one to equal you."

Responsorial Psalm (Ps 119:57, 72, 76-77, 127-128, 129-130)

R̸. (97a) Lord, I love your commands.

I have said, O LORD, that my part
    is to keep your words.
The law of your mouth is to me more precious
    than thousands of gold and silver pieces.

R̸. Lord, I love your commands.

Let your kindness comfort me
    according to your promise to your servants.
Let your compassion come to me that I may live,
    for your law is my delight.

R̸. Lord, I love your commands.

For I love your commands
    more than gold, however fine.
For in all your precepts I go forward;
    every false way I hate.

R̸. Lord, I love your commands.

Wonderful are your decrees;
    therefore I observe them.
The revelation of your words sheds light,
    giving understanding to the simple.

R̸. Lord, I love your commands.

Second Reading (Rom 8:28-30)

Reflecting on Living the Gospel

"The kingdom of heaven is like . . ." What motivates the actions of the person, merchant, and fishermen is that they have already come upon the extreme good which they seek: the treasure in the field, the pearl of great price, the catch of fish. They have encountered the treasure they desire; now they do what they must to have it. So it is with us. We have already come upon the extreme good which we spend our lives seeking: the kingdom of heaven. The challenge is to give our all to attain it.

Connecting the Responsorial Psalm to the Readings

With 176 verses, Psalm 119 is the longest of the psalms. It contains twenty-two sections, each beginning with a successive letter of the Hebrew alphabet. Within each section there are eight verses, each beginning with the letter assigned to that section. Furthermore, the psalm uses eight terms for the Law: way, law, decrees, commands, precepts, statutes, ordinances, words. It is clear that Psalm 119 is an extended meditation on the Law, not intended to be prayed in one sitting, but savored, section by section, over the course of a lifetime.

The use of verses from Psalm 119 on this Sunday suggests that the Law itself is a treasure of great price and rich reward, a guide to discernment of what is good and true, a storeroom of wisdom old and new (gospel). Solomon's request for "an understanding heart" (first reading) could only have come from one for whom the Law was already a source of strength and a guide to discernment. In singing this psalm we, too, acknowledge God's Law as the guide of our lives and the treasure of our hearts.

Psalmist Preparation

As you prepare to sing this Sunday's psalm, spend some time examining how you see God's Law. Do you see the Law as a list of "dos and don'ts" which put limits on what you would like to have and to do, or do you see it as a guide to rich, relational living? Your answer depends on where you believe true treasure lies. Pray for the grace to look where Solomon looks and to see what Jesus sees.

Prayer

Loving God, you give us your law to teach us wisdom and understanding. Lead us to treasure its guidance that we may come to love you and one another with freedom and fullness. We ask this through Christ our Lord. Amen.

Gospel (Matt 14:13-21; L112A)

When Jesus heard of the death of John the Baptist, he withdrew in a boat to a deserted place by himself. The crowds heard of this and followed him on foot from their towns. When he disembarked and saw the vast

crowd, his heart was moved with pity for them, and he cured their sick. When it was evening, the disciples approached him and said, "This is a deserted place and it is already late; dismiss the crowds so that they can go to the villages and buy food for themselves." Jesus said to them, "There is no need for them to go away; give them some food yourselves." But they said to him, "Five loaves and two fish are all we have here." Then he said, "Bring them here to me," and he ordered the crowds to sit down on the grass. Taking the five loaves and the two fish, and looking up to heaven, he said the blessing, broke the loaves, and gave them to the disciples, who in turn gave them to the crowds. They all ate and were satisfied, and they picked up the fragments left over—twelve wicker baskets full. Those who ate were about five thousand men, not counting women and children.

First Reading (Isa 55:1-3)

Thus says the LORD:
> All you who are thirsty,
> come to the water!
> You who have no money,
> come, receive grain and eat;
> come, without paying and without cost,
> drink wine and milk!
> Why spend your money for what is not bread;
> your wages for what fails to satisfy?
> Heed me, and you shall eat well,
> you shall delight in rich fare.
> Come to me heedfully,
> listen, that you may have life.
> I will renew with you the everlasting covenant,
> the benefits assured to David.

Responsorial Psalm (Ps 145:8-9, 15-16, 17-18)

R̸. (cf. 16) The hand of the Lord feeds us; he answers all our needs.

The LORD is gracious and merciful,
  slow to anger and of great kindness.
The LORD is good to all
  and compassionate toward all his works.

R̸. The hand of the Lord feeds us; he answers all our needs.

The eyes of all look hopefully to you,
  and you give them their food in due season;
you open your hand
  and satisfy the desire of every living thing.

R̸. The hand of the Lord feeds us; he answers all our needs.

The LORD is just in all his ways
  and holy in all his works.
The LORD is near to all who call upon him,
  to all who call upon him in truth.

R̸. The hand of the Lord feeds us; he answers all our needs.

Second Reading (Rom 8:35, 37-39)

Reflecting on Living the Gospel
Jesus tells the disciples to "give them food yourselves." But the disciples cannot satisfy the crowds' hunger until they give Jesus all they have—a meager five loaves and two fish. Jesus blesses these gifts and returns them to the disciples who then have enough to feed the crowds, even with "fragments left over." It is not the meager resources we have which count, but what Jesus can do with these resources when we give all we have to him. With Jesus' power and blessing, the disciples (and we) can do what they cannot do on their own.

Connecting the Responsorial Psalm to the Readings
The first reading, gospel, and responsorial psalm for this Sunday all reveal a God who gives drink to the thirsty and food to the hungry not because they have earned it, but because that is the way of God. In the Isaiah reading God invites us to drink "without paying" and to feast on "rich fare." The psalm tells us that God is the sustainer of all, the One who satisfies "the desire of every living thing." The gospel puts human flesh on this revelation: Jesus, "moved with pity" for the crowd, feeds

them until they are satisfied. This is the God to whom we "look hopefully" (psalm). We know we are hungry, and we know that we shall be fed, for we know who God is.

Psalmist Preparation

God satisfies "the desire of every living thing" (responsorial psalm). What do you desire? How do you "look hopefully" to God for it? How can your singing of this psalm be a call to the assembly to "look hopefully" to God for all they need?

Prayer

Gracious God, in your kingdom you give us far more that we can ever expect. May we feast at your table now and always. We ask this through Christ our Lord. Amen.

Gospel (Matt 14:22-33; L115A)

After he had fed the people, Jesus made the disciples get into a boat and precede him to the other side, while he dismissed the crowds. After doing so, he went up on the mountain by himself to pray. When it was evening he was there alone. Meanwhile the boat, already a few miles offshore, was being tossed about by the waves, for the wind was against it. During the fourth watch of the night, he came toward them walking on the sea. When the disciples saw him walking on the sea they were terrified. "It is a ghost," they said, and they cried out in fear. At once Jesus spoke to them, "Take courage, it is I; do not be afraid." Peter said to him in reply, "Lord, if it is you, command me to come to you on the water." He said, "Come." Peter got out of the boat and began to walk on the water toward Jesus. But when he saw how strong the wind was he became frightened; and, beginning to sink, he cried out, "Lord, save me!" Immediately Jesus stretched out his hand and caught Peter, and said to him, "O you of little faith, why did you doubt?" After they got into the boat, the wind died down. Those who were in the boat did him homage, saying, "Truly, you are the Son of God."

First Reading (1 Kgs 19:9a, 11-13a)

At the mountain of God, Horeb, Elijah came to a cave where he took shelter. Then the LORD said to him, "Go outside and stand on the mountain before the LORD; the LORD will be passing by." A strong and heavy wind was rending the mountains and crushing rocks before the LORD— but the LORD was not in the wind. After the wind there was an earthquake— but the LORD was not in the earthquake. After the earthquake there was fire— but the LORD was not in the fire. After the fire there was a tiny whispering sound. When he heard this, Elijah hid his face in his cloak and went and stood at the entrance of the cave.

Responsorial Psalm (Ps 85:9, 10, 11-12, 13-14)

℟. (8) Lord, let us see your kindness, and grant us your salvation.

I will hear what God proclaims;
  the LORD—for he proclaims peace.
Near indeed is his salvation to those who fear him,
  glory dwelling in our land.

℟. Lord, let us see your kindness, and grant us your salvation.

Kindness and truth shall meet;
  justice and peace shall kiss.
Truth shall spring out of the earth,
  and justice shall look down from heaven.

℟. Lord, let us see your kindness, and grant us your salvation.

The LORD himself will give his benefits;
  our land shall yield its increase.
Justice shall walk before him,
  and prepare the way of his steps.

℟. Lord, let us see your kindness, and grant us your salvation.

Second Reading (Rom 9:1-5)

Reflecting on Living the Gospel
This gospel brings into sharp contrast divine action and human response, divine trustworthiness and human doubt, divine power and human weakness. When these contrasts clash, those who give themselves over to divine action are saved; those who rely on their own human response face death. This clash is evident within Peter: when he looks to Jesus and trusts him, he walks on water; when he looks away from Jesus to the frightening wind and waves, he begins to sink. All Jesus' disciples must contend with this inevitable clash.

Connecting the Responsorial Psalm to the Readings
Psalm 85 was possibly written when the Israelites returned from Babylon and found their homeland devastated. As they listened to "what God proclaims" and saw God restoring their land, their sense of hopelessness and loss became newfound confidence and joy.

The Israelites saw God draw new life out of devastation (psalm). Elijah discerned God's presence in the most insignificant phenomenon (first reading). Peter experienced Jesus pull him up from waves of sure death (gospel). No matter how crushed our spirit or depleted our resources, no matter how hard it is to discern the presence of God, no matter how grave the danger we are in, how foolhardy our ventures, or how weak our faith, God is always present and acting to save us. In this psalm we ask to see more clearly what God is doing so that we may believe more fully that God is present and acting to save.

Psalmist Preparation
In this responsorial psalm you invite the assembly—no matter what dangerous, raging waters are currently present in their lives, in the church, or in the world—to walk with confidence in God's power to save. You invite them to see the future as God envisions it. Do you yourself see this future? When are you tempted to doubt God's salvation? What or who helps you believe in God's power and care?

Prayer
God of salvation, you fulfill every promise. May we see your marvelous works, hear your silent presence, and recognize your every coming to us. We ask this through Christ our Lord. Amen.

Gospel (Luke 1:39-56; L622)

Mary set out and traveled to the hill country in haste to a town of Judah, where she entered the house of Zechariah and greeted Elizabeth. When Elizabeth heard Mary's greeting, the infant leaped in her womb, and Elizabeth, filled with the Holy Spirit, cried out in a loud voice and said, "Blessed are you among women, and blessed is the fruit of your womb. And how does this happen to me, that the mother of my Lord should come to me? For at the moment the sound of your greeting reached my ears, the infant in my womb leaped for joy. Blessed are you who believed that what was spoken to you by the Lord would be fulfilled."

And Mary said:

"My soul proclaims the greatness of the Lord;
   my spirit rejoices in God my Savior
   for he has looked upon his lowly servant.
From this day all generations will call me blessed:
   the Almighty has done great things for me,
   and holy is his Name.
   He has mercy on those who fear him
   in every generation.
He has shown the strength of his arm,
   and has scattered the proud in their conceit.
He has cast down the mighty from their thrones,
   and has lifted up the lowly.
He has filled the hungry with good things,
   and the rich he has sent away empty.
He has come to the help of his servant Israel
   for he has remembered his promise of mercy,
   the promise he made to our fathers,
   to Abraham and his children forever."

Mary remained with her about three months and then returned to her home.

First Reading (Rev 11:19a; 12:1-6a, 10ab)

God's temple in heaven was opened, and the ark of his covenant could be seen in the temple.

A great sign appeared in the sky, a woman clothed with the sun, with the moon beneath her feet, and on her head a crown of twelve stars. She was with child and wailed aloud in pain as she labored to give birth. Then another sign appeared in the sky; it was a huge red dragon, with seven heads and ten horns, and on its heads were seven diadems. Its tail swept away a third of the stars in the sky and hurled them down to the earth. Then the dragon stood before the woman about to give birth, to devour her child when she gave birth. She gave birth to a son, a male child, destined to rule all the nations with an iron rod. Her child was caught up to God and his throne. The woman herself fled into the desert where she had a place prepared by God.

Then I heard a loud voice in heaven say:
"Now have salvation and power come,
   and the Kingdom of our God
   and the authority of his Anointed One."

Responsorial Psalm (Ps 45:10, 11, 12, 16)

R̸. (10bc) The queen stands at your right hand, arrayed in gold.

The queen takes her place at your right hand in gold of Ophir.

R̸. The queen stands at your right hand, arrayed in gold.

Hear, O daughter, and see; turn your ear,
   forget your people and your father's house.

R̸. The queen stands at your right hand, arrayed in gold.

So shall the king desire your beauty;
   for he is your lord.

R̸. The queen stands at your right hand, arrayed in gold.

They are borne in with gladness and joy;
   they enter the palace of the king.

R̸. The queen stands at your right hand, arrayed in gold.

See Appendix, p. 219, for Second Reading

THE ASSUMPTION OF
THE BLESSED VIRGIN MARY

Reflecting on Living the Gospel

In the *Magnificat* Mary humbly says that "all generations will call me
blessed." Her blessedness is a reflection of her fidelity to God's plan of
salvation. Because of her own submission to God's divine plan, Elizabeth
recognizes Mary's fidelity and becomes the first of "all generations" to
call Mary blessed. Now we are the generation that calls Mary blessed.
Moreover, we too are blessed when we are faithful to God's plan of salvation, open ourselves to God's many comings, and believe that God is
doing "great things" in and through us.

Connecting the Responsorial Psalm to the Readings

Psalm 45 was a nuptial psalm used in the wedding ceremony between an
Israelite king and his bride. The people called upon the bride to forget
her family and homeland and embrace a new and more glorious relationship. She chose to do so, but not alone: with "gladness and joy" an entire
retinue followed her.

By accepting her role in the incarnation, Mary chose to embody the
cosmic struggle between the forces of evil and the saving power of God
(first reading). Blessed is she for believing in the power and promise of
God even when these seemed hidden from view (gospel). Blessed is she
for not clinging to past and present and venturing in hope into an unseen
future. Now the victory of Christ over sin and death is completed in her
(second reading) and God celebrates her beauty (psalm). In her, the lowly
have been lifted up and the hungering satisfied (gospel). In her, humanity
has been wedded to God. And we belong to the retinue.

Psalmist Preparation

As you sing this responsorial psalm, you celebrate your own entrance
into heaven for the entire church is borne with Mary into God's kingdom.
How can you prepare yourself to sing such promise and glory? How can
you imitate Mary more fully in her choice to cooperate with God's plan
for salvation?

Prayer

Glorious God, the victory of your Son over sin and death has been completed in Mary whom you raised to your right hand in heaven. May we,
like her, always say *yes* to your holy will that one day we may share in
her glory. We ask this through Christ our Lord. Amen.

Gospel (Matt 15:21-28; L118A)

At that time, Jesus withdrew to the region of Tyre and Sidon. And behold, a Canaanite woman of that district came and called out, "Have pity on me, Lord, Son of David! My daughter is tormented by a demon." But Jesus did not say a word in answer to her. Jesus' disciples came and asked him, "Send her away, for she keeps calling out after us." He said in reply, "I was sent only to the lost sheep of the house of Israel." But the woman came and did Jesus homage, saying, "Lord, help me." He said in reply, "It is not right to take the food of the children and throw it to the dogs." She said, "Please, Lord, for even the dogs eat the scraps that fall from the table of their masters." Then Jesus said to her in reply, "O woman, great is your faith! Let it be done for you as you wish." And the woman's daughter was healed from that hour.

First Reading (Isa 56:1, 6-7)

Thus says the LORD:
> Observe what is right, do what is just;
>> for my salvation is about to come,
>> my justice, about to be revealed.

> The foreigners who join themselves to the LORD,
>> ministering to him,
> loving the name of the LORD,
>> and becoming his servants—
> all who keep the sabbath free from profanation
>> and hold to my covenant,
> them I will bring to my holy mountain
>> and make joyful in my house of prayer;
> their burnt offerings and sacrifices
>> will be acceptable on my altar,
> for my house shall be called
>> a house of prayer for all peoples.

Responsorial Psalm (Ps 67:2-3, 5, 6, 8)

℟. (4) O God, let all the nations praise you!

May God have pity on us and bless us;
    may he let his face shine upon us.
So may your way be known upon earth;
    among all nations, your salvation.

℟. O God, let all the nations praise you!

May the nations be glad and exult
    because you rule the peoples in equity;
    the nations on the earth you guide.

℟. O God, let all the nations praise you!

May the peoples praise you, O God;
    may all the peoples praise you!
May God bless us,
    and may all the ends of the earth fear him!

℟. O God, let all the nations praise you!

Second Reading (Rom 11:13-15, 29-32)

Reflecting on Living the Gospel
The Canaanite woman "keeps calling out" to Jesus because she wants
him to remove the demon from her daughter—to remove the evil which
separates. Her great faith moves Jesus to grant her request. Faith, by nature, is persistent. Persistence, by nature, is single-minded. Single-
mindedness, by nature, achieves the end it seeks. Like the woman in the
gospel seeking healing for her daughter, our faith must be great enough
to overcome barriers, must focus persistently on Jesus, and must bear the
fruit of salvation and healing for others.

Connecting the Responsorial Psalm to the Readings
Psalm 67 was a song of thanksgiving for the harvest which expressed
the ever-widening reach of God's blessings: first upon the people of Israel, then upon all nations, and finally to the ends of the earth. Even during the period of the Old Testament the Israelites were beginning to see
that their election as God's chosen people was not meant to be exclusive
but to be a means of salvation for all peoples.

The first reading also proclaims that God's blessings and salvation
are for all peoples. In the gospel Jesus makes this revelation concrete

when he responds to the Canaanite woman's persistent plea and heals her daughter. In the responsorial psalm we pray that all peoples be brought into the circle of God's embrace. We expand our hearts to the reach of God's salvation. We move from the disciples wanting to dismiss a needy person who is bothering them to Jesus acclaiming her faith and answering her need. We join Jesus in fulfilling God's plan that all peoples come to salvation.

Psalmist Preparation

As you prepare to sing this responsorial psalm you might spend time reflecting on your own understanding of the reach of God's salvation. Whom do you find it hard to see within God's saving embrace? Whose cries of need seem more a bother to you than an opportunity to show God's saving care (gospel)? How, on the other hand, have you grown in your understanding and in your ability to respond? How has your heart been widened?

Prayer

Loving God, you call all peoples to salvation. Widen our hearts that we, too, may embrace all peoples, near or far, seen or unseen, known or unknown. We ask this through Christ our Lord. Amen.

Gospel (Matt 16:13-20; L121A)

Jesus went into the region of Caesarea Philippi and he asked his disciples, "Who do people say that the Son of Man is?" They replied, "Some say John the Baptist, others Elijah, still others Jeremiah or one of the prophets." He said to them, "But who do you say that I am?" Simon Peter said in reply, "You are the Christ, the Son of the living God." Jesus said to him in reply, "Blessed are you, Simon son of Jonah. For flesh and blood has not revealed this to you, but my heavenly Father. And so I say to you, you are Peter, and upon this rock I will build my church, and the gates of the netherworld shall not prevail against it. I will give you the keys to the kingdom of heaven. Whatever you bind on earth shall be bound in heaven; and whatever you loose on earth shall be loosed in heaven." Then he strictly ordered his disciples to tell no one that he was the Christ.

First Reading (Isa 22:19-23)

Thus says the LORD to Shebna, master of the palace:
"I will thrust you from your office
    and pull you down from your station.
On that day I will summon my servant
    Eliakim, son of Hilkiah;
I will clothe him with your robe,
    and gird him with your sash,
    and give over to him your authority.
He shall be a father to the inhabitants of Jerusalem,
    and to the house of Judah.
I will place the key of the House of David on Eliakim's shoulder;
    when he opens, no one shall shut;
    when he shuts, no one shall open.
I will fix him like a peg in a sure spot,
    to be a place of honor for his family."

Responsorial Psalm (Ps 138:1-2, 2-3, 6, 8)

℟. (8bc) Lord, your love is eternal; do not forsake the work of your hands.

I will give thanks to you, O LORD, with all my heart,
    for you have heard the words of my mouth;
in the presence of the angels I will sing your praise;
    I will worship at your holy temple.

℟. Lord, your love is eternal; do not forsake the work of your hands.

I will give thanks to your name,
    because of your kindness and your truth:
when I called, you answered me;
    you built up strength within me.

℟. Lord, your love is eternal; do not forsake the work of your hands.

The LORD is exalted, yet the lowly he sees,
    and the proud he knows from afar.
Your kindness, O LORD, endures forever;
    forsake not the work of your hands.

℟. Lord, your love is eternal; do not forsake the work of your hands.

Second Reading (Rom 11:33-36)

Reflecting on Living the Gospel
Jesus is not simply initiating an open discussion about his identity; he is leading the disciples to personal understanding and profession of who he is. Peter arrives there when he acclaims, "You are the Christ, the Son of the Living God." Each of us must come to this same personal profession about who Jesus is. The church is that community of individuals who have come personally to know who Jesus is and have chosen personally to make Jesus known to the world. Jesus himself will lead us there through our personal encounters with him.

Connecting the Responsorial Psalm to the Readings
In some translations of Psalm 138 the word "angels" in the first strophe is translated "other gods," for the Hebrew term used (ʾelohim) variously meant "God," "gods," or "godlike beings." These multiple meanings emerged as Israel slowly groped toward belief in one God. As their faith in the one God ʾElohim grew, they dethroned their notion of other gods. Compared to the one God, other gods were mere angels or idols, and it is

before these shadows of former power that the psalmist sings God's praises.

How fitting to sing this psalm on the Sunday when Peter recognizes who Jesus is. As with Israel his recognition was a slow process. As with Israel his movement toward faith was a gift of God's revelation. As with Israel his faith would be the foundation of the faith of many others. So, too, for us. In this psalm we thank God for revealing the divine Self to us and ask God never to forsake this work of salvation begun in us.

Psalmist Preparation

The "work of [God's] hands" about which you sing in this Sunday's psalm is the gift of revelation, the gift of faith, the gift of the church founded upon the person Peter who grew in faith through experience and grace. You could pick any one of these—revelation, faith, the church—to pray about this week. How do you, through experience and grace, hear God's revelation? grow in faith? walk with the community of the church?

Prayer

Gracious God, you call us to faith in you and your Son Jesus. May this work you have begun in us draw us together as the community of the church and lead us always to serve you. We ask this through Christ our Lord. Amen.

Gospel (Matt 16:21-27; L124A)

Jesus began to show his disciples that he must go to Jerusalem and suffer greatly from the elders, the chief priests, and the scribes, and be killed and on the third day be raised. Then Peter took Jesus aside and began to rebuke him, "God forbid, Lord! No such thing shall ever happen to you." He turned and said to Peter, "Get behind me, Satan! You are an obstacle to me. You are thinking not as God does, but as human beings do."

Then Jesus said to his disciples, "Whoever wishes to come after me must deny himself, take up his cross, and follow me. For whoever wishes to save his life will lose it, but whoever loses his life for my sake will find it. What profit would there be for one to gain the whole world and forfeit his life? Or what can one give in exchange for his life? For the Son of Man will come with his angels in his Father's glory, and then he will repay all according to his conduct."

First Reading (Jer 20:7-9)

You duped me, O LORD, and I let myself be duped;
    you were too strong for me, and you triumphed.
All the day I am an object of laughter;
    everyone mocks me.

Whenever I speak, I must cry out,
    violence and outrage is my message;
the word of the LORD has brought me
    derision and reproach all the day.

I say to myself, I will not mention him,
    I will speak in his name no more.
But then it becomes like fire burning in
    my heart,
    imprisoned in my bones;
I grow weary holding it in, I cannot endure it.

Responsorial Psalm (Ps 63:2, 3-4, 5-6, 8-9)

℟. (2b) My soul is thirsting for you, O Lord my God.

O God, you are my God whom I seek;
　　for you my flesh pines and my soul thirsts
　　like the earth, parched, lifeless and without water.

℟. My soul is thirsting for you, O Lord my God.

Thus have I gazed toward you in the sanctuary
　　to see your power and your glory,
for your kindness is a greater good than life;
　　my lips shall glorify you.

℟. My soul is thirsting for you, O Lord my God.

Thus will I bless you while I live;
　　lifting up my hands, I will call upon your name.
As with the riches of a banquet shall my soul be satisfied,
　　and with exultant lips my mouth shall praise you.

℟. My soul is thirsting for you, O Lord my God.

You are my help,
　　and in the shadow of your wings I shout for joy.
My soul clings fast to you;
　　your right hand upholds me.

℟. My soul is thirsting for you, O Lord my God.

Second Reading (Rom 12:1-2)

Reflecting on Living the Gospel
No wonder Peter rebukes Jesus! Jesus "began to show his disciples" what faithful discipleship demands: denying self, losing self, letting self die. Jesus teaches his disciples to let go of self so that a new self can be given. What we relinquish is ourselves as we are now; what we are given is a new self born from identifying completely with Jesus. It takes a lifetime of discipleship to embrace Jesus' way of living. It takes a lifetime of discipleship to let Jesus transform our life into his Life.

Connecting the Responsorial Psalm to the Readings
Jesus does not hedge the truth when he tells the disciples: I must go to Jerusalem and be killed and then raised, and you must follow in my footsteps. Peter reacts as did Jeremiah in his day: Lord, you have "duped" me; I thought we were heading for glory and now you promise degrada-

tion and death. Jeremiah cries, What kind of God are you? Peter cries, What kind of Messiah are you?

To these questions the responsorial psalm replies: You are the God for whom we thirst, the God whose kindness is "greater . . . than life" itself, the God who alone ultimately satisfies us. If we maintain our focus on this God, we will have, as did Jesus, as did Jeremiah, as ultimately did Peter, the courage to lose our life. For we will have learned that in our very thirsting for God we already taste the greater life promised us.

Psalmist Preparation

This Sunday's gospel challenges you not to be naive about discipleship: its cost is suffering and death. But you are also promised a reward that far surpasses this cost: life itself (gospel), and a love even greater than life (psalm). Can you already taste what is in store? Do you thirst for it?

Prayer

God of our longing, you alone can satisfy the deepest desires of our heart. Lead us to thirst always and only for you that we may know the fullness of life you promise us. We ask this through Christ our Lord. Amen.

Gospel (Matt 18:15-20; L127A)

Jesus said to his disciples: "If your brother sins against you, go and tell him his fault between you and him alone. If he listens to you, you have won over your brother. If he does not listen, take one or two others along with you, so that 'every fact may be established on the testimony of two or three witnesses.' If he refuses to listen to them, tell the church. If he refuses to listen even to the church, then treat him as you would a Gentile or a tax collector. Amen, I say to you, whatever you bind on earth shall be bound in heaven, and whatever you loose on earth shall be loosed in heaven. Again, amen, I say to you, if two of you agree on earth about anything for which they are to pray, it shall be granted to them by my heavenly Father. For where two or three are gathered together in my name, there am I in the midst of them."

First Reading (Ezek 33:7-9)

Thus says the LORD:

You, son of man, I have appointed watchman for the house of Israel;
when you hear me say anything, you shall warn them for me.
If I tell the wicked, "O wicked one, you shall surely die,"
and you do not speak out to dissuade the wicked from his way,
the wicked shall die for his guilt,
but I will hold you responsible for his death.
But if you warn the wicked,
trying to turn him from his way,
and he refuses to turn from his way,
he shall die for his guilt,
but you shall save yourself.

Responsorial Psalm (Ps 95:1-2, 6-7, 8-9)

R̸. (8) If today you hear his voice, harden not your hearts.

Come, let us sing joyfully to the LORD;
let us acclaim the rock of our salvation.
Let us come into his presence with thanksgiving;
let us joyfully sing psalms to him.

R̸. If today you hear his voice, harden not your hearts.

Come, let us bow down in worship;
　　let us kneel before the LORD who made us.
For he is our God,
　　and we are the people he shepherds, the flock he guides.
R̞. If today you hear his voice, harden not your hearts.

Oh, that today you would hear his voice:
　　"Harden not your hearts as at Meribah,
　　　as in the day of Massah in the desert,
　　where your fathers tempted me;
　　　they tested me though they had seen my works."
R̞. If today you hear his voice, harden not your hearts.

Second Reading (Rom 13:8-10)

Reflecting on Living the Gospel
Jesus acknowledges inevitable conflicts arising among those living in the community of the church. Rifts in relationships between members of the church are actually rifts in the relationship with Jesus himself. Healing fractures ensures that members of the church remain in relationship with Jesus and grow in love for one another. The impulse for resolving conflicts comes from Jesus himself and his continued Presence in the community. The response to Jesus must come from the members of the church and their work of reconciliation.

Connecting the Responsorial Psalm to the Readings
In Psalm 95, an enthronement psalm sung while the Israelites processed to the temple, a song leader calls the community to enter God's presence singing songs of praise and thanksgiving. In the midst of this call to worship, however, the leader sounds a jarring note: the people are warned not to turn against God as their ancestors did in the desert. The human heart, they are reminded, is fickle and easily hardened.

This Sunday the Lectionary applies Psalm 95 to us, the church. We are called to worship. We are called to hear the voice of God and heed it. But fidelity is not easy and so we are also called to confront one another honestly when we fail (first reading and gospel) and to handle the conflicts and hurts among us directly and openly (gospel). We are to deal with our fickle, human hearts with the grace promised us by Christ (gospel). At stake is the authenticity of our community and the genuineness of our worship.

Psalmist Preparation

When you sing this psalm you invite not only the community but yourself to be faithful to the challenge of Christian community. In what relationships or situations is God calling you to soften your heart and reach out in reconciliation? How is God offering you help with this?

Prayer

God of salvation, you bring us together as the community of the church. Help us to call each other to fidelity, to seek reconciliation when needed, and to support one another in love that we may reveal the presence of Christ among us. We ask this through Christ our Lord. Amen.

Gospel (John 3:13-17; L638)

Jesus said to Nicodemus:
"No one has gone up to heaven
    except the one who has come down from heaven, the Son of Man.
And just as Moses lifted up the serpent in the desert,
    so must the Son of Man be lifted up,
    so that everyone who believes in him may have eternal life."

For God so loved the world that he gave his only Son,
    so that he who believes in him might not perish
    but might have eternal life.
For God did not send his Son into the world to condemn the world,
    but that the world might be saved through him.

First Reading (Num 21:4b-9)

With their patience worn out by the journey,
    the people complained against God and Moses,
    "Why have you brought us up from Egypt to die in this desert,
    where there is no food or water?
We are disgusted with this wretched
        food!"

In punishment the LORD sent among the
        people saraph serpents,
    which bit the people so that many of
        them died.
Then the people came to Moses and
        said,
    "We have sinned in complaining
        against the LORD and you.
Pray the LORD to take the serpents from
    us."
So Moses prayed for the people, and the LORD said to Moses,
    "Make a saraph and mount it on a pole,
    and if any who have been bitten look at it, they will live."
Moses accordingly made a bronze serpent and mounted it on a pole,
    and whenever anyone who had been bitten by a serpent
    looked at the bronze serpent, he lived.

Responsorial Psalm (Ps 78:1-2, 34-35, 36-37, 38)

℟. (cf. 7b) Do not forget the works of the Lord!

Hearken, my people, to my teaching;
    incline your ears to the words of my mouth.
I will open my mouth in a parable,
    I will utter mysteries from of old.

℟. Do not forget the works of the Lord!

While he slew them they sought him
    and inquired after God again,
Remembering that God was their rock
    and the Most High God, their redeemer.

℟. Do not forget the works of the Lord!

But they flattered him with their mouths
    and lied to him with their tongues,
Though their hearts were not steadfast toward him,
    nor were they faithful to his covenant.

℟. Do not forget the works of the Lord!

Yet he, being merciful, forgave their sin
    and destroyed them not;
Often he turned back his anger
    and let none of his wrath be roused.

℟. Do not forget the works of the Lord!

See Appendix, p. 219, for Second Reading

Reflecting on Living the Gospel

The Father did not give over the Son to die, but he did give him to *us* so that we might share in his risen Life. Through the self-emptying obedience of Jesus, the cross, a sign of ignominy, becomes a sign of exaltation—not only of Jesus himself whom God lifts up in glory, but also of all of us who gaze upon the cross in faith and are lifted up to eternal Life. Jesus being lifted up on the cross means we can share in the Son's eternal glory.

Connecting the Responsorial Psalm to the Readings

The "mysteries from of old" recounted in Psalm 78 refer to God's unrelenting fidelity to the Israelites despite their infidelity and falsehood.

How often to save their own skins did they swear trumped-up allegiance to God while holding back their hearts from true conversion. Yet God never turned away from them, responding instead with mercy and forgiveness. So, too, does God turn toward us by giving "his only Son" for our salvation (gospel). Christ himself held back nothing for our sakes, emptying himself of godly power in order to take on human existence and show us the way to salvation (second reading). May we never forget what God has done for us in Christ. May we believe and be saved (gospel).

Psalmist Preparation

As you prepare to sing the salvation story told in these verses from Psalm 78, flesh out the details. When has the church turned its back on God, then been offered God's merciful forgiveness and restoration? When has our nation done the same and received the same? When have you personally? Identifying these "further details" will make the story you tell ours and not just the experience of the Israelites of long ago. Then you will understand the "mysteries from of old" about which you sing. Then you will remember what you ask the assembly never to forget (psalm refrain).

Prayer

Redeeming God, you remain faithful to us even when we turn away from you. Help us to remember always your gift of salvation in Christ Jesus, who emptied himself on the cross that we may be filled with your love and your grace. We ask this through Christ our Lord. Amen.

Gospel (Matt 20:1-16a; L133A)

Jesus told his disciples this parable: "The kingdom of heaven is like a landowner who went out at dawn to hire laborers for his vineyard. After agreeing with them for the usual daily wage, he sent them into his vineyard. Going out about nine o'clock, the landowner saw others standing idle in the marketplace, and he said to them, 'You too go into my vineyard, and I will give you what is just.' So they went off. And he went out again around noon, and around three o'clock, and did likewise. Going out about five o'clock, the landowner found others standing around, and said to them, 'Why do you stand here idle all day?' They answered, 'Because no one has hired us.' He said to them, 'You too go into my vineyard.' When it was evening the owner of the vineyard said to his foreman, 'Summon the laborers and give them their pay, beginning with the last and ending with the first.' When those who had started about five o'clock came, each received the usual daily wage. So when the first came, they thought that they would receive more, but each of them also got the usual wage. And on receiving it they grumbled against the landowner, saying, 'These last ones worked only one hour, and you have made them equal to us, who bore the day's burden and the heat.' He said to one of them in reply, 'My friend, I am not cheating you. Did you not agree with me for the usual daily wage? Take what is yours and go. What if I wish to give this last one the same as you? Or am I not free to do as I wish with my own money? Are you envious because I am generous?' Thus, the last will be first, and the first will be last."

First Reading (Isa 55:6-9)

Seek the Lord while he may be found,
  call him while he is near.
Let the scoundrel forsake his way,
  and the wicked his thoughts;
let him turn to the Lord for mercy;
  to our God, who is generous in forgiving.
For my thoughts are not your thoughts,
  nor are your ways my ways, says the Lord.

As high as the heavens are above the earth,
   so high are my ways above your ways
   and my thoughts above your thoughts.

Responsorial Psalm (Ps 145:2-3, 8-9, 17-18)

R⁊. (18a) The Lord is near to all who call upon him.

Every day will I bless you,
   and I will praise your name forever and ever.
Great is the LORD and highly to be praised;
   his greatness is unsearchable.

R⁊. The Lord is near to all who call upon him.

The LORD is gracious and merciful,
   slow to anger and of great kindness.
The LORD is good to all
   and compassionate toward all his works.

R⁊. The Lord is near to all who call upon him.

The LORD is just in all his ways
   and holy in all his works.
The LORD is near to all who call upon him,
   to all who call upon him in truth.

R⁊. The Lord is near to all who call upon him.

Second Reading (Phil 1:20c-24, 27a)

Reflecting on Living the Gospel
This gospel raises the question of who is first and who is last in the
kingdom of heaven. Those laborers are last who shift their focus from
doing the work of the landowner to grumbling about the amount of
wages others are receiving. Those are first who do not labor in the vineyard because of the amount of wages, but simply because they are privi-
leged to share in the work of the landowner. Indeed, simply being called
to the privilege of sharing in Jesus' work of salvation is its own
recompense.

Connecting the Responsorial Psalm to the Readings
Like a parent sitting at a child's bedside, ready to respond to the slightest
cry, God is ever near, answering our every need (psalm refrain). Once we
recognize that God is giving us all that we need, we no longer find ourselves grumbling about what God is giving to others (gospel). Instead we

rejoice that everyone's needs are being met and bless the One who is "just in all his ways" (psalm). We turn away from rivalries with one another to celebrate the limitless expanse of God's care and generosity. Then the "ways" and "thoughts" of God that are far above us (first reading) can find a place very near, in our own hearts. May this be what we call upon God to give us (refrain).

Psalmist Preparation

"The Lord is near to all . . . who call upon him in truth" (psalm). What truth about God is this psalm and these readings inviting you to ponder? What truth about yourself? How during this week might you call upon God to show you this truth more clearly?

Prayer

Nearby God, your mercy and generosity far surpass what our tight-bound hearts can ever imagine. Help us draw near to you that we may see as you see, think as you think, and give of ourselves as you do. We ask this through Christ our Lord. Amen.

SEPTEMBER 28, 2014

Gospel (Matt 21:28-32; L136A)

Jesus said to the chief priests and elders of the people: "What is your opinion? A man had two sons. He came to the first and said, 'Son, go out and work in the vineyard today.' He said in reply, 'I will not,' but afterwards changed his mind and went. The man came to the other son and gave the same order. He said in reply, 'Yes, sir,' but did not go. Which of the two did his father's will?" They answered,

"The first." Jesus said to them, "Amen, I say to you, tax collectors and prostitutes are entering the kingdom of God before you. When John came to you in the way of righteousness, you did not believe him; but tax collectors and prostitutes did. Yet even when you saw that, you did not later change your minds and believe him."

First Reading (Ezek 18:25-28)

Thus says the LORD:
You say, "The LORD's way is not fair!"
Hear now, house of Israel:
    Is it my way that is unfair, or rather, are not your ways unfair?
When someone virtuous turns away from virtue to commit iniquity, and
    dies,
    it is because of the iniquity he committed that he must die.
But if he turns from the wickedness he has committed,
    and does what is right and just,
    he shall preserve his life;
    since he has turned away from all the sins that he has committed,
    he shall surely live, he shall not die.

Responsorial Psalm (Ps 25:4-5, 6-7, 8-9)

R℣. (6a) Remember your mercies, O Lord.

Your ways, O LORD, make known to me;
    teach me your paths,
guide me in your truth and teach me,
    for you are God my savior.

R℣. Remember your mercies, O Lord.

Remember that your compassion, O Lord,
  and your love are from of old.
The sins of my youth and my frailties remember not;
    in your kindness remember me,
    because of your goodness, O Lord.

R⁊. Remember your mercies, O Lord.

Good and upright is the Lord;
  thus he shows sinners the way.
He guides the humble to justice,
  and teaches the humble his way.

R⁊. Remember your mercies, O Lord.

Second Reading (Phil 2:1-11 [or Phil 2:1-5])

Reflecting on Living the Gospel
The first son's initial answer to his father was honest (he never intended
to be obedient), but he "changed his mind" and did what his father asked.
By contrast, the second son's seemingly obedient "Yes, sir" in fact was
dishonest—he "did not go." Jesus condemns the chief priests and elders'
behavior because of their own utter dishonesty. The sinful tax collectors
and prostitutes (like the first son) change their behavior. Trapped in their
self-righteousness, the chief priests and elders (like the second son) refuse to change. Changing—choosing conversion of self—is a matter of
utter honesty with self, God, and others.

Connecting the Responsorial Psalm to the Readings
The first reading and gospel this Sunday point out that we have a tenu-
ous hold on righteousness and easily fluctuate between "yes" and "no" to
God. But the responsorial psalm indicates that God never wavers in the
offer of forgiveness. Psalm 25 invites us to turn our attention from our
own behavior to the goodness and mercy of God. Upheld by such mercy
we can admit our sins of yesterday (psalm) and seek the conversion we
need (first reading). We have only to ask and God will teach us what we
need to know to live rightly (psalm). The point is not to worry about
being sinners (that is inevitable) but to be humble and honest enough to
be teachable. The tax collectors and prostitutes in the gospel have been
great learners; the self-righteous chief priest and elders, on the other
hand, have learned nothing. God never stops inviting us to a change of
heart. It rests upon us to learn what God is teaching us.

Psalmist Preparation

What do these verses from Psalm 25 reveal about God's manner of relating to us? In what manner does it invite us to relate to God? On a personal level, what ways do you need to ask God to teach you? How is God doing this teaching?

Prayer

Gracious God, in sending your Son Jesus, you say "yes" to us. Help us always to say "yes" to you, not just in word but also in deed. We ask this through Christ our Lord. Amen.

Gospel (Matt 21:33-43; L139A)

Jesus said to the chief priests and the elders of the people: "Hear another parable. There was a landowner who planted a vineyard, put a hedge around it, dug a wine press in it, and built a tower. Then he leased it to tenants and went on a journey. When vintage time drew near, he sent his servants to the tenants to obtain his produce. But the tenants seized the ser-

vants and one they beat, another they killed, and a third they stoned. Again he sent other servants, more numerous than the first ones, but they treated them in the same way. Finally, he sent his son to them, thinking, 'They will respect my son.' But when the tenants saw the son, they said to one another, 'This is the heir. Come, let us kill him and acquire his inheritance.' They seized him, threw him out of the vineyard, and killed him. What will the owner of the vineyard do to those tenants when he comes?" They answered him, "He will put those wretched men to a wretched death and lease his vineyard to other tenants who will give him the produce at the proper times." Jesus said to them, "Did you never read in the Scriptures:

> *The stone that the builders rejected*
> *has become the cornerstone;*
> *by the Lord has this been done,*
> *and it is wonderful in our eyes?*

Therefore, I say to you, the kingdom of God will be taken away from you and given to a people that will produce its fruit."

First Reading (Isa 5:1-7)

> Let me now sing of my friend,
> my friend's song concerning his vineyard.
> My friend had a vineyard
> on a fertile hillside;
> he spaded it, cleared it of stones,
> and planted the choicest vines;
> within it he built a watchtower,
> and hewed out a wine press.
> Then he looked for the crop of grapes,
> but what it yielded was wild grapes.

Now, inhabitants of Jerusalem and people of Judah,
    judge between me and my vineyard:
What more was there to do for my vineyard
    that I had not done?
Why, when I looked for the crop of grapes,
    did it bring forth wild grapes?
Now, I will let you know
    what I mean to do with my vineyard:
take away its hedge, give it to grazing,
    break through its wall, let it be trampled!
Yes, I will make it a ruin:
    it shall not be pruned or hoed,
    but overgrown with thorns and briers;
I will command the clouds
    not to send rain upon it.
The vineyard of the LORD of hosts is the house of Israel,
    and the people of Judah are his cherished plant;
he looked for judgment, but see, bloodshed!
    for justice, but hark, the outcry!

Responsorial Psalm (Ps 80:9, 12, 13-14, 15-16, 19-20)

R̸. (Isaiah 5:7a) The vineyard of the Lord is the house of Israel.

A vine from Egypt you transplanted;
    you drove away the nations and planted it.
It put forth its foliage to the Sea,
    its shoots as far as the River.

R̸. The vineyard of the Lord is the house of Israel.

Why have you broken down its walls,
    so that every passer-by plucks its fruit,
the boar from the forest lays it waste,
    and the beasts of the field feed upon it?

R̸. The vineyard of the Lord is the house of Israel.

Once again, O LORD of hosts,
    look down from heaven, and see;
take care of this vine,
    and protect what your right hand has planted,
    the son of man whom you yourself made strong.

R̸. The vineyard of the Lord is the house of Israel.

Then we will no more withdraw from you;
  give us new life, and we will call upon your name.
O LORD, God of hosts, restore us;
  if your face shine upon us, then we shall be saved.

R℣. The vineyard of the Lord is the house of Israel.

Second Reading (Phil 4:6-9)

Reflecting on Living the Gospel
The "chief priests and elders," by their own words, align themselves
with the tenants in the parable—these Jewish leaders are unfaithful and
ultimately they, too, kill the One God sends into the vineyard. Even more,
they seal their own death when they answer Jesus that those violent tenants will be killed. The "death" of the "chief priests and elders" will be
that "the kingdom of God," the vine of Life, will be taken away from
them. Those who are faithful and accept the Son receive the Life only
God's kingdom can bring. They receive the very Life of God.

Connecting the Responsorial Psalm to the Readings
For the past two Sundays we have reflected in the responsorial psalms
on God's eternal mercy. This Sunday, however, the psalm confronts us
with God's righteous judgment and punishment. Despite the teachings
of the Law, the words of the prophets, and the coming of God in the
flesh of Jesus, the chosen people have repeatedly turned from righteousness. What more could I have done for you? God cries (first reading).

Please do more, we cry in response (psalm). Save us once again and
we will return to you. The psalms themselves have trained us in this
frame of mind, for they have taught us, O God, that you are merciful and
good, forgiving to the last degree. Do not let the kingdom be taken from
us (although we deserve it) but give us again the chance we need to produce the fruit you so desire (gospel). Need we doubt God's response?

Psalmist Preparation
As you sing this responsorial psalm you pronounce God's righteous
judgment against Israel (and the church) for infidelity and you beg God
to offer them one more chance. You promise that if this new chance is
granted the people will respond with conversion of heart and renewed fidelity. This is a story God has heard many times before. You need to feel
God's frustration. You need to feel the people's contrition. And you need
to believe that the new chance you beg for will be granted.

Prayer

God of infinite mercy, you judge rightly that we have turned away from you. Call us back that we may stand again within your presence and your embrace. We ask this through Christ our Lord. Amen.

Gospel (Matt 22:1-14 [or shorter form Matt 22:1-10]; L142A)

Jesus again in reply spoke to the chief priests and elders of the people in parables, saying, "The kingdom of heaven may be likened to a king who gave a wedding feast for his son. He dispatched his servants to summon the invited guests to the feast, but they refused to come. A second time he sent other servants, saying, 'Tell those invited: "Behold, I have prepared my banquet, my calves and fattened cattle are killed, and everything is ready; come to the feast."'" Some ignored the invitation and went away, one to his farm, another to his business. The rest laid hold of his servants, mistreated them, and killed them. The king was enraged and sent his troops, destroyed those murderers, and burned their city. Then he said to his servants, 'The feast is ready, but those who were invited were not worthy to come. Go out, therefore, into the main roads and invite to the feast whomever you find.' The servants went out into the streets and gathered all they found, bad and good alike, and the hall was filled with guests. But when the king came in to meet the guests, he saw a man there not dressed in a wedding garment. The king said to him, 'My friend, how is it that you came in here without a wedding garment?' But he was reduced to silence. Then the king said to his attendants, 'Bind his hands and feet, and cast him into the darkness outside, where there will be wailing and grinding of teeth.' Many are invited, but few are chosen."

First Reading (Isa 25:6-10a)

On this mountain the LORD of hosts
    will provide for all peoples
a feast of rich food and choice wines,
    juicy, rich food and pure, choice wines.
On this mountain he will destroy
    the veil that veils all peoples,
the web that is woven over all nations;
    he will destroy death forever.
The Lord GOD will wipe away
    the tears from every face;

the reproach of his people he will remove
   from the whole earth; for the LORD has spoken.
On that day it will be said:
"Behold our God, to whom we looked to save us!
   This is the LORD for whom we looked;
   let us rejoice and be glad that he has saved us!"
For the hand of the LORD will rest on this mountain.

Responsorial Psalm (Ps 23:1-3a, 3b-4, 5, 6)

R̸. (6cd) I shall live in the house of the Lord all the days of my life.

The LORD is my shepherd; I shall not want.
   In verdant pastures he gives me repose;
beside restful waters he leads me;
   he refreshes my soul.

R̸. I shall live in the house of the Lord all the days of my life.

He guides me in right paths
   for his name's sake.
Even though I walk in the dark valley
   I fear no evil; for you are at my side
with your rod and your staff
   that give me courage.

R̸. I shall live in the house of the Lord all the days of my life.

You spread the table before me
   in the sight of my foes;
you anoint my head with oil;
   my cup overflows.

R̸. I shall live in the house of the Lord all the days of my life.

Only goodness and kindness follow me
   all the days of my life;
and I shall dwell in the house of the LORD
   for years to come.

R̸. I shall live in the house of the Lord all the days of my life.

Second Reading (Phil 4:12-14, 19-20)

Reflecting on Living the Gospel

The king is adamant about filling the wedding hall with guests. His initial guest list has been carefully drawn up, but when these invited guests do not come, the king sends his servants out to invite anyone and everyone—the "bad and good alike." The hall must be filled. There can be no real feast with only a partially filled hall—the joy and happiness of the feast must be full. In the same manner as the parable king, God persistently invites us to the royal banquet in the "kingdom of heaven."

Connecting the Responsorial Psalm to the Readings

Psalm 23 sings of absolute trust in God who shepherds, guides, heals, and nourishes. The psalmist has no doubt of being protected and of receiving fullness of life from the Lord. Such confidence correlates perfectly with Isaiah's vision of the day when God will destroy all evil, wipe away all tears, and provide a feast "for all peoples" (first reading). Yet the behaviors of those invited to the banquet in the gospel contradict these sentiments. A feast has been spread for them—sumptuous and free—yet they refuse to come. Why would anyone say no to such a feast?

The first reading and psalm simply intensify the gospel contrast between the persistence of God in calling people to the fullness of life and their refusal to respond. We know from personal experience how real and repetitive this refusal can be. And we know from Psalm 23 how real and persistent God's corrective guidance will be.

Psalmist Preparation

The refrain for this Sunday's responsorial psalm can be interpreted as both a promise (on God's part) and a pledge (on our part). In what area of your life is God calling you right now to keep your pledge to live as one who belongs to God's house?

Prayer

Shepherd God, you call us to the messianic banquet of your Son Jesus. May we accept your invitation without hesitation and run to the feast with joy. We ask this through Christ our Lord. Amen.

Gospel (Matt 22:15-21; L145A)

The Pharisees went off and plotted how they might entrap Jesus in speech. They sent their disciples to him, with the Herodians, saying, "Teacher, we know that you are a truthful man and that you teach the way of God in accordance with the truth. And you are not concerned with anyone's opinion, for you do not regard a person's status. Tell us, then, what is your opinion: Is it  lawful to pay the census tax to Caesar or not?" Knowing their malice, Jesus said, "Why are you testing me, you hypocrites? Show me the coin that pays the census tax." Then they handed him the Roman coin. He said to them, "Whose image is this and whose inscription?" They replied, "Caesar's." At that he said to them, "Then repay to Caesar what belongs to Caesar and to God what belongs to God."

First Reading (Isa 45:1, 4-6)

Thus says the LORD to his anointed, Cyrus,
    whose right hand I grasp,
subduing nations before him,
    and making kings run in his service,
opening doors before him
    and leaving the gates unbarred:
For the sake of Jacob, my servant,
    of Israel, my chosen one,
I have called you by your name,
    giving you a title, though you knew me not.
I am the LORD and there is no other,
    there is no God besides me.
It is I who arm you, though you know me not,
    so that toward the rising and the setting of the sun
    people may know that there is none besides me.
I am the LORD, there is no other.

Responsorial Psalm (Ps 96:1, 3, 4-5, 7-8, 9-10)

R̸. (7b) Give the Lord glory and honor.

Sing to the LORD a new song;
  sing to the LORD, all you lands.
Tell his glory among the nations;
  among all peoples, his wondrous deeds.

R̸. Give the Lord glory and honor.

For great is the LORD and highly to be praised;
  awesome is he, beyond all gods.
For all the gods of the nations are things of nought,
  but the LORD made the heavens.

R̸. Give the Lord glory and honor.

Give to the LORD, you families of nations,
  give to the LORD glory and praise;
  give to the LORD the glory due his name!
Bring gifts, and enter his courts.

R̸. Give the Lord glory and honor.

Worship the LORD, in holy attire;
  tremble before him, all the earth;
say among the nations: The LORD is king,
  he governs the peoples with equity.

R̸. Give the Lord glory and honor.

Second Reading (1 Thess 1:1-5b)

Reflecting on Living the Gospel

Jesus is not fooled by the Pharisees and Herodians' shameful flattery, but sees through it to their malice and hypocrisy. These vices lead to a false dichotomy between earthly and divine kingdoms. Goodness and truth lead us to recognize our place and proper conduct in both kingdoms. When earthly kingdoms are guided by God's values and ways, they are no less than the spatial presence here and now of God's kingdom. And we pay only one tax: the self-giving that bears the image of Jesus.

Connecting the Responsorial Psalm to the Readings

The connection between the verses of Psalm 96 and this Sunday's first reading and gospel is readily evident. God alone is God; even when un-recognized God alone is the source of all power and authority (first reading). The psalm calls us to give God "glory and praise" and to announce God's sovereignty to all nations. Jesus repeats this command in his admonition to the Pharisees: give God proper due (gospel).

But a subtle irony in the readings lends even greater weight to this command of Jesus. While Cyrus, a non-Jew, unknowingly unfolds God's plan, the Pharisees, acknowledged religious leaders among the Jews, knowingly work to subvert it. One who does not know God furthers God's redemptive plan while those reputed to be God's servants thwart it. The message for us is that to give God proper due it is not sufficient merely to mouth praise or to engage in public religious activity. Rather, we must give what Cyrus is unaware of and the Pharisees refuse: our hearts in conscious cooperation with God's will.

Psalmist Preparation

The greatest "glory and honor" we can give God is an obedient heart. This is what you call the assembly to in singing Psalm 96. Is there anything which stands in the way of your own making of this self-gift?

Prayer

God of salvation, despite human ways and wiles you are bringing your plan of salvation to fulfillment. Lead us, like Jesus, to remain always loyal to you and to cooperate with your will in all that we do. We ask this through Christ our Lord. Amen.

Gospel (Matt 22:34-40; L148A)

When the Pharisees heard that Jesus had silenced the Sadducees, they gathered together, and one of them, a scholar of the law, tested him by asking, "Teacher, which commandment in the law is the greatest?" He said to him, "You shall love the Lord, your God, with all your heart, with all your soul, and with all your mind. This is the greatest and the first commandment. The second is like it: You shall love your neighbor as yourself. The whole law and the prophets depend on these two commandments."

First Reading (Exod 22:20-26)

Thus says the LORD:
"You shall not molest or oppress an alien,
　for you were once aliens yourselves in the land of Egypt.
You shall not wrong any widow or orphan.
If ever you wrong them and they cry out to me,
　I will surely hear their cry.
My wrath will flare up, and I will kill you with the sword;
　then your own wives will be widows, and your children orphans.

"If you lend money to one of your poor neighbors among my people,
　you shall not act like an extortioner toward him
　by demanding interest from him.
If you take your neighbor's cloak as a pledge,
　you shall return it to him before sunset;
　for this cloak of his is the only covering he has for his body.
What else has he to sleep in?
If he cries out to me, I will hear him; for I am compassionate."

Responsorial Psalm (Ps 18:2-3, 3-4, 47, 51)

℞. (2) I love you, Lord, my strength.

I love you, O LORD, my strength,
　O LORD, my rock, my fortress, my deliverer.

℞. I love you, Lord, my strength.

My God, my rock of refuge,
  my shield, the horn of my salvation, my stronghold!
Praised be the LORD, I exclaim,
  and I am safe from my enemies.
℟. I love you, Lord, my strength.

The LORD lives and blessed be my rock!
  Extolled be God my savior.
You who gave great victories to your king
  and showed kindness to your anointed.
℟. I love you, Lord, my strength.

Second Reading (1 Thess 1:5c-10)

Reflecting on Living the Gospel
By asking "which commandment in the law is the greatest," the Pharisees reveal an attitude toward law far different from that of Jesus. Instead of limiting the demand of the law as the Pharisees do to discrete
commandments that are kept or not, Jesus teaches that the demand of
the law embraces the totality of our relationships with God, self, and
neighbor. Love defines our relationships; love is the wellspring of obedience to any commandment. Love is the greatest commandment because
it truly is the whole Law of God.

Connecting the Responsorial Psalm to the Readings
Implied in this responsorial psalm's expression of wholehearted love of
God ("I love you, Lord, my strength") is acknowledgment that the source
of our capacity to love both God and neighbor unselfishly and unstint-
ingly is God. It is God who gives us the strength to live according to the
demands of the covenant. The first reading spells out these demands in
concrete terms as acts of compassion toward real people in real need. In
the gospel Jesus teaches us that fidelity to the covenant rests as much
upon these acts of compassion as it does upon love of God.
    This command to love wholeheartedly and concretely is demanding.
The good news of the psalm is that we are not left to our own meager resources. Rather we draw on a reserve that is divine, unshakable, and unfailing. We can love as we are commanded because God is "[our] strength."

Psalmist Preparation
You can love God with all your heart and soul and you can love your
neighbor as yourself (gospel) because God gives you the strength to do

so (psalm). You might take time this week to reflect on how this strength has grown in you and give God thanks. You might also examine where this strength needs to grow and ask for God's grace.

Prayer

God of love, you command us to love you with our whole being and to love our neighbor as we love ourselves. Give us the strength we need to keep our covenant with you by putting this love into concrete action. We ask this through Christ our Lord. Amen.

Gospel (Matt 5:1-12a; L667)

When Jesus saw the crowds, he went up the mountain, and after he had sat down, his disciples came to him. He began to teach them, saying:

"Blessed are the poor in spirit,
   for theirs is the Kingdom of heaven.
Blessed are they who mourn,
   for they will be comforted.
Blessed are the meek,
   for they will inherit the land.
Blessed are they who hunger and thirst
    for righteousness,
   for they will be satisfied.
Blessed are the merciful,
   for they will be shown mercy.
Blessed are the clean of heart,
   for they will see God.
Blessed are the peacemakers,
   for they will be called children of God.
Blessed are they who are persecuted for the sake of righteousness,
   for theirs is the Kingdom of heaven.
Blessed are you when they insult you and persecute you
   and utter every kind of evil against you falsely because of me.
Rejoice and be glad,
   for your reward will be great in heaven."

First Reading (Rev 7:2-4, 9-14)

I, John, saw another angel come up from the East, holding the seal of the living God. He cried out in a loud voice to the four angels who were given power to damage the land and the sea, "Do not damage the land or the sea or the trees until we put the seal on the foreheads of the servants of our God." I heard the number of those who had been marked with the seal, one hundred and forty-four thousand marked from every tribe of the children of Israel.

After this I had a vision of a great multitude, which no one could count, from every nation, race, people, and tongue. They stood before the throne and before the Lamb, wearing white robes and holding palm branches in their hands. They cried out in a loud voice:

"Salvation comes from our God, who is seated on the throne, and from
the Lamb."

All the angels stood around the throne and around the elders and the four living creatures. They prostrated themselves before the throne, worshiped God, and exclaimed:

"Amen. Blessing and glory, wisdom and thanksgiving,
honor, power, and might
be to our God forever and ever. Amen."

Then one of the elders spoke up and said to me, "Who are these wearing white robes, and where did they come from?" I said to him, "My lord, you are the one who knows." He said to me, "These are the ones who have survived the time of great distress; they have washed their robes and made them white in the Blood of the Lamb."

Responsorial Psalm (Ps 24:1-2, 3-4, 5-6)

℟. (cf. 6) Lord, this is the people that longs to see your face.

The LORD's are the earth and its fullness;
the world and those who dwell in it.
For he founded it upon the seas
and established it upon the rivers.

℟. Lord, this is the people that longs to see your face.

Who can ascend the mountain of the LORD?
or who may stand in his holy place?
One whose hands are sinless, whose heart is clean,
who desires not what is vain.

℟. Lord, this is the people that longs to see your face.

He shall receive a blessing from the LORD,
a reward from God his savior.
Such is the race that seeks for him,
that seeks the face of the God of Jacob.

℟. Lord, this is the people that longs to see your face.

See Appendix, p. 219, for Second Reading

Reflecting on Living the Gospel

The whole gamut of human emotions and needs Jesus "saw [in] the crowds" prompted him to teach his disciples the Beatitudes. Nine times Jesus uses the word "Blessed" in reference to the crowds. Rather than the prevailing notion that those who are blessed by God are wealthy, healthy, and prosperous, Jesus reveals that blessedness lies in the dignity and goodness of the person as person. The challenge of the gospel is for us to live up to this dignity and goodness.

Connecting the Responsorial Psalm to the Readings

Psalm 24 is one of the psalms of ascent. As the Israelites traveled to Jerusalem for solemn festival they raised their eyes to the "mountain of the Lord." Upon arrival at the temple door, they were questioned, "Who can ascend [this] mountain . . . who may stand in [this] holy place?" They then responded, "One whose hands are sinless, whose heart is clean, who desires not what is vain." These are the very qualities Jesus spells out in the Beatitudes (gospel). The Israelites were faithful to the law and the covenant because they knew they were God's chosen people. We live the Beatitudes because we know we are God's children (second reading). With the Israelites, we long to see God's face (psalm refrain). With all those who faithfully pursue this longing, we reap the reward of heaven.

Psalmist Preparation

The first psalm strophe tells of God's power, the last of God's blessings upon those who are faithful. The middle strophe describes those who are faithful. In singing this psalm you speak sometimes to God, sometimes to the people. Pray that you may speak to both with humility and love.

Prayer

Good and gracious God, you bestow upon us great love, calling us your own children. Teach us to live always as your holy ones, faithful to your ways of blessedness. We ask this through Christ our Lord. Amen.

Gospel (John 6:37-40; L668.8)

Jesus said to the crowds:

"Everything that the Father gives me will
come to me,
and I will not reject anyone who comes to
me,
because I came down from heaven not to do
my own will
but the will of the one who sent me.
And this is the will of the one who sent me,
that I should not lose anything of what he
gave me,
but that I should raise it on the last day.
For this is the will of my Father,
that everyone who sees the Son and believes in him
may have eternal life,
and I shall raise him up on the last day."

*Additional reading choices may be found in the Lectionary for Mass,
L668.*

First Reading (Wis 3:1-9)

The souls of the just are in the hand of God,
and no torment shall touch them.
They seemed, in the view of the foolish, to be dead;
and their passing away was thought an affliction
and their going forth from us, utter destruction.
But they are in peace.
For if before men, indeed they be punished,
yet is their hope full of immortality;
chastised a little, they shall be greatly blessed,
because God tried them
and found them worthy of himself.
As gold in the furnace, he proved them,
and as sacrificial offerings he took them to himself.
In the time of their visitation they shall shine,
and shall dart about as sparks through stubble;
they shall judge nations and rule over peoples,
and the Lord shall be their King forever.

Those who trust in him shall understand truth,
    and the faithful shall abide with him in love:
because grace and mercy are with his holy ones,
    and his care is with his elect.

Responsorial Psalm (Ps 23:1-3a, 3b-4, 5, 6; L668.1)

℟. (1a) The Lord is my shepherd; there is nothing I shall want.

    or:

℟. Though I walk in the valley of darkness, I fear no evil, for you are
with me.

The LORD is my shepherd; I shall not want.
    In verdant pastures he gives me repose;
beside restful waters he leads me;
    he refreshes my soul.

℟. The Lord is my shepherd; there is nothing I shall want.

    or:

℟. Though I walk in the valley of darkness, I fear no evil, for you are
with me.

He guides me in right paths
    for his name's sake.
Even though I walk in the dark valley
    I fear no evil; for you are at my side
with your rod and your staff
    that give me courage.

℟. The Lord is my shepherd; there is nothing I shall want.

    or:

℟. Though I walk in the valley of darkness, I fear no evil, for you are
with me.

You spread the table before me
    in the sight of my foes;
You anoint my head with oil;
    my cup overflows.

℟. The Lord is my shepherd; there is nothing I shall want.

    or:

℟. Though I walk in the valley of darkness, I fear no evil, for you are
with me.

Only goodness and kindness follow me
    all the days of my life;
and I shall dwell in the house of the LORD
    for years to come.

℟. The Lord is my shepherd; there is nothing I shall want.
    or:

℟. Though I walk in the valley of darkness, I fear no evil, for you are
with me.

See Appendix, p. 219, for Second Reading

Reflecting on Living the Gospel

God wills that all "have eternal life." While this gift is surely and freely
given by God, it nonetheless requires something of us: belief in the Son.
Rather than an intellectual consent, this belief is a consent of our self, of
our will, of our life. Jesus will raise up on the "last day" those who come
to him, who choose to be grasped by him, and who welcome the Life he
gives. These are the faithful departed who rest in peace and whom we
commemorate this day.

Connecting the Responsorial Psalm to the Readings

Psalm 23, perhaps the best known and most beloved psalm in the psalter,
speaks of the "dark valley" through which all of us must walk on our
way to eternal Life. That valley is death. We do not know from direct experience what lies on the other side, but the psalm describes a banquet
table, a healing anointing, and an eternal home with God. The psalm also
provides the hope we need as we traverse this inevitable journey from
birth through death to new Life. We are guided and protected on the way
by a Shepherd who, having already made the journey, is no longer subject to death (second reading). He is surefooted and will lose no one along
the way (gospel). And so we sing today, not in mourning, but with quiet
confidence in the One who saves from death. We know he holds fast all
our beloved who have gone before us on this journey. We know he will
hold us fast when it is our turn to make the crossing.

Psalmist Preparation

Whether you sing the first refrain offered or the second, you represent
the community of the church standing on the edge of death without fear.
You stand before the assembly as an embodiment of hope in God's

promise of resurrection. What feeds this hope in you? How can you effectively communicate it to the assembly?

Prayer

God of Life, you lead us through death to fullness of Life. May the faithful departed who have gone before us in death rest in the peace of your presence and may we who remain stand firm in the hope of your promise. We ask this through Christ our Lord. Amen.

Gospel (John 2:13-22; L671)

Since the Passover of the Jews was near,
    Jesus went up to Jerusalem.
He found in the temple area those who
        sold oxen, sheep, and doves,
    as well as the money-changers seated
        there.

He made a whip out of cords
    and drove them all out of the temple
        area, with the sheep and oxen,
    and spilled the coins of the
        money-changers
    and overturned their tables,
    and to those who sold doves he said,
    "Take these out of here,
    and stop making my Father's house a marketplace."
His disciples recalled the words of Scripture,
    Zeal for your house will consume me.
At this the Jews answered and said to him,
    "What sign can you show us for doing this?"
Jesus answered and said to them,
    "Destroy this temple and in three days I will raise it up."
The Jews said,
    "This temple has been under construction for forty-six years,
    and you will raise it up in three days?"
But he was speaking about the temple of his Body.
Therefore, when he was raised from the dead,
    his disciples remembered that he had said this,
    and they came to believe the Scripture
    and the word Jesus had spoken.

First Reading (Ezek 47:1-2, 8-9, 12)

The angel brought me
    back to the entrance of the temple,
    and I saw water flowing out
    from beneath the threshold of the temple toward the east,
    for the façade of the temple was toward the east;
    the water flowed down from the southern side of the temple,
    south of the altar.

He led me outside by the north gate,
  and around to the outer gate facing the east,
  where I saw water trickling from the southern side.
He said to me,
"This water flows into the eastern district down upon the Arabah,
  and empties into the sea, the salt waters, which it makes fresh.
Wherever the river flows,
  every sort of living creature that can multiply shall live,
  and there shall be abundant fish,
  for wherever this water comes the sea shall be made fresh.
Along both banks of the river, fruit trees of every kind shall grow;
  their leaves shall not fade, nor their fruit fail.
Every month they shall bear fresh fruit,
  for they shall be watered by the flow from the sanctuary.
Their fruit shall serve for food, and their leaves for medicine."

Responsorial Psalm (Ps 46:2-3, 5-6, 8-9)

R̰. (5) The waters of the river gladden the city of God, the holy dwelling
of the Most High.

God is our refuge and our strength,
  an ever-present help in distress.
Therefore, we fear not, though the earth be shaken
  and mountains plunge into the depths of the sea.

R̰. The waters of the river gladden the city of God, the holy dwelling of
the Most High.

There is a stream whose runlets gladden the city of God,
  the holy dwelling of the Most High.
God is in its midst; it shall not be disturbed;
  God will help it at the break of dawn.

R̰. The waters of the river gladden the city of God, the holy dwelling of
the Most High.

The LORD of hosts is with us;
  our stronghold is the God of Jacob.
Come! behold the deeds of the Lord,
  the astounding things he has wrought on earth.

R̰. The waters of the river gladden the city of God, the holy dwelling of
the Most High.

THE DEDICATION OF THE LATERAN BASILICA

See Appendix, p. 220, for Second Reading

Reflecting on Living the Gospel

Jesus' zeal exceeds merely cleansing the temple. His zeal is for the people to be faithful to their covenant with God. His zeal did lead ultimately to the destruction of his body on the cross. But it also brought the Father on the third day to raise him to new Life. This feast day of our mother church in Rome calls us to a zeal that will consume us when we give our lives for others as Jesus did and live the new Life given to us by the Father.

Connecting the Responsorial Psalm to the Readings

In the design, strength, and beauty of the city of Jerusalem and its temple the Israelites saw the power of God overcoming the forces of chaos and destruction which threatened their life and well-being. Psalm 46 expressed their certainty that God dwelt in their midst as stronghold and refuge. Ezekiel describes water flowing from the temple in an unending stream of life and fruitfulness (first reading). Jesus identifies the true temple as his body which will rise from the destruction of death to new life (gospel). Paul calls us the temple, God's holy people built on the foundation which is Christ (second reading).

This solemnity celebrates that God's dwelling place on earth is not a building made of stone, but a community of disciples born from the death of Christ and the life-giving waters of baptism. As God's living and breathing dwelling place, we are a source of life for all the world. We need only to drink deeply and often of the water God has set flowing within us (see psalm refrain).

Psalmist Preparation

To gain better understanding of the responsorial psalm chosen for this solemnity, read the full text of Psalm 46 from which it is taken. Notice especially the contrast between the raging waters of destruction and the life-giving waters which flow from the city of God. Reflecting on the psalm and these readings will help you see that what you sing about is much more than a basilica in Rome. You sing about the church, the people who are God's dwelling on earth, the community from whom God's life-giving water flows out to all the world.

Prayer

God of grace, you have made the community of the church your dwelling place on earth. Keep us always faithful to our baptism that we may be living stones from whom the waters of your salvation will flow out to all the world. We ask this through Christ our Lord. Amen.

NOVEMBER 16, 2014

Gospel (Matt 25:14-30 [or shorter form Matt 25:14-15, 19-21; L157A)

Jesus told his disciples this parable: "A man going on a journey called in his servants and entrusted his possessions to them. To one he gave five talents; to another, two; to a third, one— to each according to his ability. Then he went away. Immediately the one who received five talents went and traded with them, and made another five. Likewise, the one who received two made another two. But the

man who received one went off and dug a hole in the ground and buried his master's money.

"After a long time the master of those servants came back and settled accounts with them. The one who had received five talents came forward bringing the additional five. He said, 'Master, you gave me five talents. See, I have made five more.' His master said to him, 'Well done, my good and faithful servant. Since you were faithful in small matters, I will give you great responsibilities. Come, share your master's joy.' Then the one who had received two talents also came forward and said, 'Master, you gave me two talents. See, I have made two more.' His master said to him, 'Well done, my good and faithful servant. Since you were faithful in small matters, I will give you great responsibilities. Come, share your master's joy.' Then the one who had received the one talent came forward and said, 'Master, I knew you were a demanding person, harvesting where you did not plant and gathering where you did not scatter; so out of fear I went off and buried your talent in the ground. Here it is back.' His master said to him in reply, 'You wicked, lazy servant! So you knew that I harvest where I did not plant and gather where I did not scatter? Should you not then have put my money in the bank so that I could have got it back with interest on my return? Now then! Take the talent from him and give it to the one with ten. For to everyone who has, more will be given and he will grow rich; but from the one who has not, even what he has will be taken away. And throw this useless servant into the darkness outside, where there will be wailing and grinding of teeth.'"

THIRTY-THIRD SUNDAY IN ORDINARY TIME

First Reading (Prov 31:10-13, 19-20, 30-31)

When one finds a worthy wife,
　　her value is far beyond pearls.
Her husband, entrusting his heart to her,
　　has an unfailing prize.
She brings him good, and not evil,
　　all the days of her life.
She obtains wool and flax
　　and works with loving hands.
She puts her hands to the distaff,
　　and her fingers ply the spindle.
She reaches out her hands to the poor,
　　and extends her arms to the needy.
Charm is deceptive and beauty fleeting;
　　the woman who fears the LORD is to be praised.
Give her a reward for her labors,
　　and let her works praise her at the city gates.

Responsorial Psalm (Ps 128:1-2, 3, 4-5)

R̷. (cf. 1a) Blessed are those who fear the Lord.

Blessed are you who fear the LORD,
　　who walk in his ways!
For you shall eat the fruit of your handiwork;
　　blessed shall you be, and favored.

R̷. Blessed are those who fear the Lord.

Your wife shall be like a fruitful vine
　　in the recesses of your home;
your children like olive plants
　　around your table.

R̷. Blessed are those who fear the Lord.

Behold, thus is the man blessed
　　who fears the LORD.
The LORD bless you from Zion:
　　may you see the prosperity of Jerusalem
　　all the days of your life.

R̷. Blessed are those who fear the Lord.

Second Reading (1 Thess 5:1-6)

Reflecting on Living the Gospel

Every servant in this gospel parable is given riches by the master with the expectation that each servant will increase what has been given. Even one talent was a significant amount of riches. To bury it was to waste its potential. The wealth each of us has been given by our Master is a share in his very Life. Even a small amount is an incalculable richness. We will be judged by how we have chosen to allow this Life to increase, to grow within us. To choose otherwise is to bury our very selves.

Connecting the Responsorial Psalm to the Readings

Together the first reading and psalm offer a balanced image of a woman and a man who, each in their respective social roles, is faithful to God's desires about the manner of human living. Both texts are couched in the domestic terms which characterized much of Hebrew life and understanding, but the Lectionary's intent is to use them as a model or pattern for all sorts of lifestyles, vocations, and situations in life. In both cases the one who "fears the Lord" is faithful in carrying out the ordinary everyday demands of covenant living. She/he cares not only for those for whom they are responsible, but also reaches out to whomever is in need (first reading). For both, the fidelity and generosity of their way of living flows back to them in abundant blessings. And Jesus tells us that the greatest blessing is a share in God's own joy (gospel). May our singing of this psalm be a confident acknowledgment that we have been given the "talent" to live in this way, and that we already experience its blessedness.

Psalmist Preparation

The text of this responsorial psalm can be off-putting unless you see it in conjunction with the first reading and gospel. The Lectionary's choice of this psalm is not to elevate the role of husband over wife (although Hebrew thought and culture would have done so at the time the psalm was written) but to celebrate the blessedness which comes to any person who is faithful in daily living and ordinary relationships to the demands of discipleship. As you prepare to sing it, spend some time reflecting on the discipleship demands of daily living and ordinary relationships which belong to your life. How are you being faithful? How are you blessed because of your fidelity?

Prayer

Generous God, you have called us to build up your kingdom and gifted us with talent to do so. Keep us faithful to the commission you have given us that Christ may greet us with joy when he returns. We ask this through Christ our Lord. Amen.

NOVEMBER 23, 2014

Gospel (Matt 25:31-46; L160A)

Jesus said to his disciples: "When the Son of Man comes in his glory, and all the angels with him, he will sit upon his glorious throne, and all the nations will be assembled before him. And he will separate them one from another, as a shepherd separates the sheep from the goats. He will place the sheep on his right and the goats on his left. Then the king will say to those on his right, 'Come, you who are blessed by my Father. Inherit the kingdom prepared for you from the foundation of the world. For I was hungry and you gave me food, I was thirsty and you gave me

drink, a stranger and you welcomed me, naked and you clothed me, ill and you cared for me, in prison and you visited me.' Then the righteous will answer him and say, 'Lord, when did we see you hungry and feed you, or thirsty and give you drink? When did we see you a stranger and welcome you, or naked and clothe you? When did we see you ill or in prison, and visit you?' And the king will say to them in reply, 'Amen, I say to you, whatever you did for one of the least brothers of mine, you did for me.' Then he will say to those on his left, 'Depart from me, you accursed, into the eternal fire prepared for the devil and his angels. For I was hungry and you gave me no food, I was thirsty and you gave me no drink, a stranger and you gave me no welcome, naked and you gave me no clothing, ill and in prison, and you did not care for me.' Then they will answer and say, 'Lord, when did we see you hungry or thirsty or a stranger or naked or ill or in prison, and not minister to your needs?' He will answer them, 'Amen, I say to you, what you did not do for one of these least ones, you did not do for me.' And these will go off to eternal punishment, but the righteous to eternal life."

First Reading (Ezek 34:11-12, 15-17)

Thus says the Lord GOD:
   I myself will look after and tend my sheep.
As a shepherd tends his flock
   when he finds himself among his scattered sheep,
   so will I tend my sheep.

I will rescue them from every place where they were scattered
  when it was cloudy and dark.
I myself will pasture my sheep;
  I myself will give them rest, says the Lord GOD.
The lost I will seek out,
  the strayed I will bring back,
  the injured I will bind up,
  the sick I will heal,
  but the sleek and the strong I will destroy,
  shepherding them rightly.

As for you, my sheep, says the Lord GOD,
  I will judge between one sheep and another,
  between rams and goats.

Responsorial Psalm (Ps 23:1-2, 2-3, 5-6)

R̸. (1) The Lord is my shepherd; there is nothing I shall want.

The LORD is my shepherd; I shall not want.
  In verdant pastures he gives me repose.

R̸. The Lord is my shepherd; there is nothing I shall want.

Beside restful waters he leads me;
  he refreshes my soul.
He guides me in right paths
  for his name's sake.

R̸. The Lord is my shepherd; there is nothing I shall want.

You spread the table before me
  in the sight of my foes;
you anoint my head with oil;
  my cup overflows.

R̸. The Lord is my shepherd; there is nothing I shall want.

Only goodness and kindness follow me
  all the days of my life;
and I shall dwell in the house of the LORD
  for years to come.

R̸. The Lord is my shepherd; there is nothing I shall want.

See Appendix, p. 220, for Second Reading

Reflecting on Living the Gospel

We tend to think of Christ's final coming in judgment only in terms of the end of time. Jesus surprises us with this revelation: "When the Son of Man comes . . ." *is now in others*, no matter what their guise or condition. There is an urgency about *now*: how we respond here and now to others bears eternal consequences. There is a propinquity about *who*: the person near us is Christ and how we respond determines how we will be judged.

Connecting the Responsorial Psalm to the Readings

Coupled with the first reading Psalm 23 reveals that what God expects us to do for others (gospel) God is already always doing for us. We can seek the lost, bring back the strayed, bind up the wounded, heal the sick (first reading), give drink to the thirsty and feed the hungry (psalm) because God does these things for us. In the gospel people, good and bad, are surprised to discover that their neighbor in need was Christ. The first reading and psalm add the astounding implication that in their compassionate behavior the good were Godlike.

In the gospel Jesus announces that we will be judged according to whether we have treated others with the same care, kindness, and concern that God has treated us. We will discover both who our neighbor is (Christ) and who we are (Godlike). And we will discover where our shepherd God has been leading us all along: not to a place but to a way of being where we know the identity of one another and our oneness with God. What more could we want?

Psalmist Preparation

Our shepherd God is continually leading you forward to a new way of being and relating. Are you willing to follow?

Prayer

Saving God, you shepherd us in ways of life and love. Lead us to recognize your Son in our neighbor in need that we may become more like him and be judged worthy to enter his kingdom with joy. We ask this through Christ our Lord. Amen.

APPENDIX

FIRST SUNDAY OF ADVENT, December 1, 2013
Second Reading **(Rom 13:11-14)**

Brothers and sisters: You know the time; it is the hour now for you to awake from sleep. For our salvation is nearer now than when we first believed; the night is advanced, the day is at hand. Let us then throw off the works of darkness and put on the armor of light; let us conduct ourselves properly as in the day, not in orgies and drunkenness, not in promiscuity and lust, not in rivalry and jealousy. But put on the Lord Jesus Christ, and make no provision for the desires of the flesh.

SECOND SUNDAY OF ADVENT, December 8, 2013
Second Reading **(Rom 15:4-9)**

Brothers and sisters: Whatever was written previously was written for our instruction, that by endurance and by the encouragement of the Scriptures we might have hope. May the God of endurance and encouragement grant you to think in harmony with one another, in keeping with Christ Jesus, that with one accord you may with one voice glorify the God and Father of our Lord Jesus Christ.

Welcome one another, then, as Christ welcomed you, for the glory of God. For I say that Christ became a minister of the circumcised to show God's truthfulness, to confirm the promises to the patriarchs, but so that the Gentiles might glorify God for his mercy. As it is written:

> *Therefore, I will praise you among the Gentiles*
> *and sing praises to your name.*

THE IMMACULATE CONCEPTION OF THE BLESSED VIRGIN MARY, December 9, 2013
Second Reading **(Eph 1:3-6, 11-12)**

Brothers and sisters: Blessed be the God and Father of our Lord Jesus Christ, who has blessed us in Christ with every spiritual blessing in the heavens, as he chose us in him, before the foundation of the world, to be holy and without blemish before him. In love he destined us for adoption to himself through Jesus Christ, in accord with the favor of his will, for the praise of the glory of his grace that he granted us in the beloved.

In him we were also chosen, destined in accord with the purpose of the One who accomplishes all things according to the intention of his will, so that we might exist for the praise of his glory, we who first hoped in Christ.

THIRD SUNDAY OF ADVENT, December 15, 2013
Second Reading **(Jas 5:7-10)**

Be patient, brothers and sisters, until the coming of the Lord. See how the farmer waits for the precious fruit of the earth, being patient with it until it receives the early and the late rains. You too must be patient. Make your hearts firm, because the coming of the Lord is at hand. Do not complain, brothers and sisters, about one another, that you may not be judged. Behold, the Judge is standing before the gates. Take as an example of hardship and patience, brothers and sisters, the prophets who spoke in the name of the Lord.

FOURTH SUNDAY OF ADVENT, December 22, 2013
Second Reading (Rom 1:1-7)

Paul, a slave of Christ Jesus, called to be an apostle and set apart for the gospel of God, which he promised previously through his prophets in the holy Scriptures, the gospel about his Son, descended from David according to the flesh, but established as Son of God in power according to the Spirit of holiness through resurrection from the dead, Jesus Christ our Lord. Through him we have received the grace of apostleship, to bring about the obedience of faith, for the sake of his name, among all the Gentiles, among whom are you also, who are called to belong to Jesus Christ; to all the beloved of God in Rome, called to be holy. Grace to you and peace from God our Father and the Lord Jesus Christ.

THE NATIVITY OF THE LORD, *Vigil Mass*, December 24, 2013
Second Reading (Acts 13:16-17, 22-25)

When Paul reached Antioch in Pisidia and entered the synagogue, he stood up, motioned with his hand, and said, "Fellow Israelites and you others who are God-fearing, listen. The God of this people Israel chose our ancestors and exalted the people during their sojourn in the land of Egypt. With uplifted arm he led them out of it. Then he removed Saul and raised up David as king; of him he testified, 'I have found David, son of Jesse, a man after my own heart; he will carry out my every wish.' From this man's descendants God, according to his promise, has brought to Israel a savior, Jesus. John heralded his coming by proclaiming a baptism of repentance to all the people of Israel; and as John was completing his course, he would say, 'What do you suppose that I am? I am not he. Behold, one is coming after me; I am not worthy to unfasten the sandals of his feet.'"

THE NATIVITY OF THE LORD, *Mass at Midnight*, December 25, 2013
Second Reading (Titus 2:11-14)

Beloved: The grace of God has appeared, saving all and training us to reject godless ways and worldly desires and to live temperately, justly, and devoutly in this age, as we await the blessed hope, the appearance of the glory of our great God and savior Jesus Christ, who gave himself for us to deliver us from all lawlessness and to cleanse for himself a people as his own, eager to do what is good.

THE NATIVITY OF THE LORD, *Mass at Dawn*, December 25, 2013
Second Reading (Titus 3:4-7)

Beloved:

> When the kindness and generous love
>   of God our savior appeared,
> not because of any righteous deeds we had done
>   but because of his mercy,
> he saved us through the bath of rebirth
>   and renewal by the Holy Spirit,
> whom he richly poured out on us
>   through Jesus Christ our savior,
> so that we might be justified by his grace
>   and become heirs in hope of eternal life.

THE NATIVITY OF THE LORD, *Mass During the Day,* December 25, 2013
Second Reading (Heb 1:1-6)

Brothers and sisters: In times past, God spoke in partial and various ways to our ancestors through the prophets; in these last days, he has spoken to us through the Son, whom he made heir of all things and through whom he created the universe,

who is the refulgence of his glory, the very imprint of his being,
and who sustains all things by his mighty word.
When he had accomplished purification from sins,
he took his seat at the right hand of the Majesty on high,
as far superior to the angels
as the name he has inherited is more excellent than theirs.

For to which of the angels did God ever say:

You are my son; this day I have begotten you?

Or again:

I will be a father to him, and he shall be a son to me?

And again, when he leads the firstborn into the world, he says:

Let all the angels of God worship him.

THE HOLY FAMILY OF JESUS, MARY, AND JOSEPH, December 29, 2013
Second Reading (Col 3:12-21 [or Col 3:12-17])

Brothers and sisters: Put on, as God's chosen ones, holy and beloved, heartfelt compassion, kindness, humility, gentleness, and patience, bearing with one another and forgiving one another, if one has a grievance against another; as the Lord has forgiven you, so must you also do. And over all these put on love, that is, the bond of perfection. And let the peace of Christ control your hearts, the peace into which you were also called in one body. And be thankful. Let the word of Christ dwell in you richly, as in all wisdom you teach and admonish one another, singing psalms, hymns, and spiritual songs with gratitude in your hearts to God. And whatever you do, in word or in deed, do everything in the name of the Lord Jesus, giving thanks to God the Father through him.

Wives, be subordinate to your husbands, as is proper in the Lord. Husbands, love your wives, and avoid any bitterness toward them. Children, obey your parents in everything, for this is pleasing to the Lord. Fathers, do not provoke your children, so they may not become discouraged.

SOLEMNITY OF MARY, THE HOLY MOTHER OF GOD,
January 1, 2014
Second Reading (Gal 4:4-7)

Brothers and sisters: When the fullness of time had come, God sent his Son, born of a woman, born under the law, to ransom those under the law, so that we might receive adoption as sons. As proof that you are sons, God sent the Spirit of his Son into our hearts, crying out, "Abba, Father!" So you are no longer a slave but a son, and if a son then also an heir, through God.

THE EPIPHANY OF THE LORD, January 5, 2014
Second Reading (Eph 3:2-3a, 5-6)

Brothers and sisters: You have heard of the stewardship of God's grace that was given to me for your benefit, namely, that the mystery was made known to me by revelation. It was not made known to people in other generations as it has now been revealed to his holy apostles and prophets by the Spirit: that the Gentiles are coheirs, members of the same body, and copartners in the promise in Christ Jesus through the gospel.

THE BAPTISM OF THE LORD, January 12, 2014
Second Reading (Acts 10:34-38)

Peter proceeded to speak to those gathered in the house of Cornelius, saying: "In truth, I see that God shows no partiality. Rather, in every nation whoever fears him and acts uprightly is acceptable to him. You know the word that he sent to the Israelites as he proclaimed peace through Jesus Christ, who is Lord of all, what has happened all over Judea, beginning in Galilee after the baptism that John preached, how God anointed Jesus of Nazareth with the Holy Spirit and power. He went about doing good and healing all those oppressed by the devil, for God was with him."

THE PRESENTATION OF THE LORD, February 2, 2014
Second Reading (Heb 2:14-18)

Since the children share in blood and flesh, Jesus likewise shared in them, that through death he might destroy the one who has the power of death, that is, the Devil, and free those who through fear of death had been subject to slavery all their life. Surely he did not help angels but rather the descendants of Abraham; therefore, he had to become like his brothers and sisters in every way, that he might be a merciful and faithful high priest before God to expiate the sins of the people. Because he himself was tested through what he suffered, he is able to help those who are being tested.

ASH WEDNESDAY, March 5, 2014
Second Reading (2 Cor 5:20–6:2)

Brothers and sisters: We are ambassadors for Christ, as if God were appealing through us. We implore you on behalf of Christ, be reconciled to God. For our sake he made him to be sin who did not know sin, so that we might become the righteousness of God in him.

Working together, then, we appeal to you not to receive the grace of God in vain. For he says:

In an acceptable time I heard you,
and on the day of salvation I helped you.

Behold, now is a very acceptable time; behold, now is the day of salvation.

FIRST SUNDAY OF LENT, March 9, 2014
Second Reading (Rom 5:12-19 [or Rom 5:12, 17-19])

Brothers and sisters: Through one man sin entered the world, and through sin, death, and thus death came to all men, inasmuch as all sinned— for up to the time of the law, sin was in the world, though sin is not accounted when there is no law. But death reigned from Adam to Moses, even over those who did not sin after the pattern of the trespass of Adam, who is the type of the one who was to come.

But the gift is not like the transgression. For if by the transgression of the one, the many died, how much more did the grace of God and the gracious gift of the one man Jesus Christ overflow for the many. And the gift is not like the result of the one who sinned. For after one sin there was the judgment that brought condemnation; but the gift, after many transgressions, brought acquittal. For if, by the transgression of the one, death came to reign through that one, how much more will those who receive the abundance of grace and of the gift of justification come to reign in life through the one Jesus Christ. In conclusion, just as through one transgression condemnation came upon all, so, through one righteous act, acquittal and life came to all. For just as through the disobedience of the one man the many were made sinners, so, through the obedience of the one, the many will be made righteous.

SECOND SUNDAY OF LENT, March 16, 2014
Second Reading (2 Tim 1:8b-10)
Beloved: Bear your share of hardship for the gospel with the strength that comes from God.

He saved us and called us to a holy life, not according to our works but according to his own design and the grace bestowed on us in Christ Jesus before time began, but now made manifest through the appearance of our savior Christ Jesus, who destroyed death and brought life and immortality to light through the gospel.

THIRD SUNDAY OF LENT, March 23, 2014
Second Reading (Rom 5:1-2, 5-8)
Brothers and sisters: Since we have been justified by faith, we have peace with God through our Lord Jesus Christ, through whom we have gained access by faith to this grace in which we stand, and we boast in hope of the glory of God.

And hope does not disappoint, because the love of God has been poured out into our hearts through the Holy Spirit who has been given to us. For Christ, while we were still helpless, died at the appointed time for the ungodly. Indeed, only with difficulty does one die for a just person, though perhaps for a good person one might even find courage to die. But God proves his love for us in that while we were still sinners Christ died for us.

FOURTH SUNDAY OF LENT, March 30, 2014
Second Reading (Eph 5:8-14)
Brothers and sisters: You were once darkness, but now you are light in the Lord. Live as children of light, for light produces every kind of goodness and righteousness and truth. Try to learn what is pleasing to the Lord. Take no part in the fruitless works of darkness; rather expose them, for it is shameful even to mention the things done by them in secret; but everything exposed by the light becomes visible, for everything that becomes visible is light. Therefore, it says: / "Awake, O sleeper, / and arise from the dead, / and Christ will give you light."

FIFTH SUNDAY OF LENT, April 6, 2014
Second Reading (Rom 8:8-11)
Brothers and sisters: Those who are in the flesh cannot please God. But you are not in the flesh; on the contrary, you are in the spirit, if only the Spirit of God dwells in you. Whoever does not have the Spirit of Christ does not belong to him.

But if Christ is in you, although the body is dead because of sin, the spirit is alive because of righteousness. If the Spirit of the One who raised Jesus from the dead dwells in you, the One who raised Christ from the dead will give life to your mortal bodies also, through his Spirit dwelling in you.

PALM SUNDAY OF THE PASSION OF THE LORD, April 13, 2014
Second Reading (Phil 2:6-11)

Christ Jesus, though he was in the form of God,
    did not regard equality with God
    something to be grasped.
Rather, he emptied himself,
    taking the form of a slave,
    coming in human likeness;
    and found human in appearance,
    he humbled himself,
    becoming obedient to the point of death,
        even death on a cross.
Because of this, God greatly exalted him
    and bestowed on him the name
    which is above every name,
    that at the name of Jesus
    every knee should bend,
    of those in heaven and on earth and under the earth,
    and every tongue confess that
    Jesus Christ is Lord,
    to the glory of God the Father.

HOLY THURSDAY EVENING MASS OF THE LORD'S SUPPER, April 17, 2014
Second Reading (1 Cor 11:23-26)

Brothers and sisters: I received from the Lord what I also handed on to you, that the Lord Jesus, on the night he was handed over, took bread, and, after he had given thanks, broke it and said, "This is my body that is for you. Do this in remembrance of me." In the same way also the cup, after supper, saying, "This cup is the new covenant in my blood. Do this, as often as you drink it, in remembrance of me." For as often as you eat this bread and drink the cup, you proclaim the death of the Lord until he comes.

GOOD FRIDAY OF THE LORD'S PASSION, April 18, 2014
Second Reading (Heb 4:14-16; 5:7-9)

Brothers and sisters: Since we have a great high priest who has passed through the heavens, Jesus, the Son of God, let us hold fast to our confession. For we do not have a high priest who is unable to sympathize with our weaknesses, but one who has similarly been tested in every way, yet without sin. So let us confidently approach the throne of grace to receive mercy and to find grace for timely help.

In the days when Christ was in the flesh, he offered prayers and supplications with loud cries and tears to the one who was able to save him from death, and he was heard because of his reverence. Son though he was, he learned obedience from what he suffered; and when he was made perfect, he became the source of eternal salvation for all who obey him.

EASTER SUNDAY, April 20, 2014
Second Reading (I Cor 5:6b-8 [or Col 3:1-4])

Brothers and sisters: Do you not know that a little yeast leavens all the dough? Clear out the old yeast, so that you may become a fresh batch of dough, inasmuch as you are unleavened. For our paschal lamb, Christ, has been sacrificed. Therefore, let us celebrate the feast, not with the old yeast, the yeast of malice and wickedness, but with the unleavened bread of sincerity and truth.

SECOND SUNDAY OF EASTER, April 27, 2014
Second Reading (I Pet 1:3-9)

Blessed be the God and Father of our Lord Jesus Christ, who in his great mercy gave us a new birth to a living hope through the resurrection of Jesus Christ from the dead, to an inheritance that is imperishable, undefiled, and unfading, kept in heaven for you who by the power of God are safeguarded through faith, to a salvation that is ready to be revealed in the final time. In this you rejoice, although now for a little while you may have to suffer through various trials, so that the genuineness of your faith, more precious than gold that is perishable even though tested by fire, may prove to be for praise, glory, and honor at the revelation of Jesus Christ. Although you have not seen him you love him; even though you do not see him now yet believe in him, you rejoice with an indescribable and glorious joy, as you attain the goal of your faith, the salvation of your souls.

THIRD SUNDAY OF EASTER, May 4, 2014
Second Reading (I Pet 1:17-21)

Beloved: If you invoke as Father him who judges impartially according to each one's works, conduct yourselves with reverence during the time of your sojourning, realizing that you were ransomed from your futile conduct, handed on by your ancestors, not with perishable things like silver or gold but with the precious blood of Christ as of a spotless unblemished lamb.

He was known before the foundation of the world but revealed in the final time for you, who through him believe in God who raised him from the dead and gave him glory, so that your faith and hope are in God.

FOURTH SUNDAY OF EASTER, May 11, 2014
Second Reading (I Pet 2:20b-25)

Beloved: If you are patient when you suffer for doing what is good, this is a grace before God. For to this you have been called, because Christ also suffered for you, leaving you an example that you should follow in his footsteps.

He committed no sin, and no deceit was found in his mouth.

When he was insulted, he returned no insult; when he suffered, he did not threaten; instead, he handed himself over to the one who judges justly. He himself bore our sins in his body upon the cross, so that, free from sin, we might live for righteousness. By his wounds you have been healed. For you had gone astray like sheep, but you have now returned to the shepherd and guardian of your souls.

FIFTH SUNDAY OF EASTER, May 18, 2014
Second Reading (1 Pet 2:4-9)

Beloved: Come to him, a living stone, rejected by human beings but chosen and precious in the sight of God, and, like living stones, let yourselves be built into a spiritual house to be a holy priesthood to offer spiritual sacrifices acceptable to God through Jesus Christ. For it says in Scripture:

Behold, I am laying a stone in Zion,
a cornerstone, chosen and precious,
and whoever believes in it shall not be put to shame.

Therefore, its value is for you who have faith, but for those without faith:

The stone that the builders rejected
has become the cornerstone,

and

A stone that will make people stumble,
and a rock that will make them fall.

They stumble by disobeying the word, as is their destiny.

You are "a chosen race, a royal priesthood, a holy nation, a people of his own, so that you may announce the praises" of him who called you out of darkness into his wonderful light.

SIXTH SUNDAY OF EASTER, May 25, 2014
Second Reading (1 Pet 3:15-18)

Beloved: Sanctify Christ as Lord in your hearts. Always be ready to give an explanation to anyone who asks you for a reason for your hope, but do it with gentleness and reverence, keeping your conscience clear, so that, when you are maligned, those who defame your good conduct in Christ may themselves be put to shame. For it is better to suffer for doing good, if that be the will of God, than for doing evil. For Christ also suffered for sins once, the righteous for the sake of the unrighteous, that he might lead you to God. Put to death in the flesh, he was brought to life in the Spirit.

THE ASCENSION OF THE LORD, May 29 or June 1, 2014
Second Reading (Eph 1:17-23)

Brothers and sisters: May the God of our Lord Jesus Christ, the Father of glory, give you a Spirit of wisdom and revelation resulting in knowledge of him. May the eyes of your hearts be enlightened, that you may know what is the hope that belongs to his call, what are the riches of glory in his inheritance among the holy ones, and what is the surpassing greatness of his power for us who believe, in accord with the exercise of his great might, which he worked in Christ, raising him from the dead and seating him at his right hand in the heavens, far above every principality, authority, power, and dominion, and every name that is named not only in this age but also in the one to come. And he put all things beneath his feet and gave him as head over all things to the church, which is his body, the fullness of the one who fills all things in every way.

SEVENTH SUNDAY OF EASTER, June 1, 2014
Second Reading (1 Pet 4:13-16)

Beloved: Rejoice to the extent that you share in the sufferings of Christ, so that when his glory is revealed you may also rejoice exultantly. If you are insulted for the name of Christ, blessed are you, for the Spirit of glory and of God rests upon you. But let no one among you be made to suffer as a murderer, a thief, an evil-doer, or as an intriguer. But whoever is made to suffer as a Christian should not be ashamed but glorify God because of the name.

PENTECOST SUNDAY, June 8, 2014
Second Reading (1 Cor 12:3b-7, 12-13)

Brothers and sisters: No one can say, "Jesus is Lord," except by the Holy Spirit.

There are different kinds of spiritual gifts but the same Spirit; there are different forms of service but the same Lord; there are different workings but the same God who produces all of them in everyone. To each individual the manifestation of the Spirit is given for some benefit.

As a body is one though it has many parts, and all the parts of the body, though many, are one body, so also Christ. For in one Spirit we were all baptized into one body, whether Jews or Greeks, slaves or free persons, and we were all given to drink of one Spirit.

THE SOLEMNITY OF THE MOST HOLY TRINITY, June 15, 2014
Second Reading (2 Cor 13:11-13)

Brothers and sisters, rejoice. Mend your ways, encourage one another, agree with one another, live in peace, and the God of love and peace will be with you. Greet one another with a holy kiss. All the holy ones greet you.

The grace of the Lord Jesus Christ and the love of God and the fellowship of the Holy Spirit be with all of you.

THE SOLEMNITY OF THE MOST HOLY BODY AND BLOOD OF CHRIST, June 22, 2014
Second Reading (1 Cor 10:16-17)

Brothers and sisters: The cup of blessing that we bless, is it not a participation in the blood of Christ? The bread that we break, is it not a participation in the body of Christ? Because the loaf of bread is one, we, though many, are one body, for we all partake of the one loaf.

SAINTS PETER AND PAUL, APOSTLES, June 29, 2014
Second Reading (2 Tim 4:6-8, 17-18)

I, Paul, am already being poured out like a libation, and the time of my departure is at hand. I have competed well; I have finished the race; I have kept the faith. From now on the crown of righteousness awaits me, which the Lord, the just judge, will award to me on that day, and not only to me, but to all who have longed for his appearance.

The Lord stood by me and gave me strength, so that through me the proclamation might be completed and all the Gentiles might hear it. And I was rescued from the lion's mouth. The Lord will rescue me from every evil threat and will bring me safe to his heavenly Kingdom. To him be glory forever and ever. Amen.

THE ASSUMPTION OF THE BLESSED VIRGIN MARY, August 15, 2014
Second Reading **(1 Cor 15:20-27)**
Brothers and sisters: Christ has been raised from the dead, the firstfruits of those who have fallen asleep. For since death came through man, the resurrection of the dead came also through man. For just as in Adam all die, so too in Christ shall all be brought to life, but each one in proper order: Christ the firstfruits; then, at his coming, those who belong to Christ; then comes the end, when he hands over the Kingdom to his God and Father, when he has destroyed every sovereignty and every authority and power. For he must reign until he has put all his enemies under his feet. The last enemy to be destroyed is death, for "he subjected everything under his feet."

THE EXALTATION OF THE HOLY CROSS, September 14, 2014
Second Reading **(Phil 2:6-11)**
Brothers and sisters:
> Christ Jesus, though he was in the form of God,
>> did not regard equality with God something to be grasped.
> Rather, he emptied himself,
> taking the form of a slave,
> coming in human likeness;
> and found human in appearance,
> he humbled himself,
> becoming obedient to death,
>> even death on a cross.
Because of this, God greatly exalted him
> and bestowed on him the name
> that is above every name,
> that at the name of Jesus
> every knee should bend,
> of those in heaven and on earth and under the earth,
> and every tongue confess that
> Jesus Christ is Lord,
> to the glory of God the Father.

ALL SAINTS, November 1, 2014
Second Reading **(1 John 3:1-3)**
Beloved: See what love the Father has bestowed on us that we may be called the children of God. Yet so we are. The reason the world does not know us is that it did not know him. Beloved, we are God's children now; what we shall be has not yet been revealed. We do know that when it is revealed we shall be like him, for we shall see him as he is. Everyone who has this hope based on him makes himself pure, as he is pure.

ALL SOULS November 2, 2014
Second Reading **(Rom 6:3-9 or [Rom 5:5-11])**
Brothers and sisters: Are you unaware that we who were baptized into Christ Jesus were baptized into his death? We were indeed buried with him through baptism into death, so that, just as Christ was raised from the dead by the glory of the Father, we too might live in newness of life.

For if we have grown into union with him through a death like his, we shall also be united with him in the resurrection. We know that our old self was crucified with him, so that our sinful body might be done away with, that we might no longer be in slavery to sin. For a dead person has been absolved from sin. If, then, we have died with Christ, we believe that we shall also live with him. We know that Christ, raised from the dead, dies no more; death no longer has power over him.

THE DEDICATION OF THE LATERAN BASILICA November 9, 2014
Second Reading (1 Cor 3:9c-11, 16-17)

Brothers and sisters: You are God's building. According to the grace of God given to me, like a wise master builder I laid a foundation, and another is building upon it. But each one must be careful how he builds upon it, for no one can lay a foundation other than the one that is there, namely, Jesus Christ.

Do you not know that you are the temple of God, and that the Spirit of God dwells in you? If anyone destroys God's temple, God will destroy that person; for the temple of God, which you are, is holy.

THE SOLEMNITY OF OUR LORD JESUS CHRIST THE KING, November 23, 2014
Second Reading (1 Cor 15:20-26, 28)

Brothers and sisters: Christ has been raised from the dead, the firstfruits of those who have fallen asleep. For since death came through man, the resurrection of the dead came also through man. For just as in Adam all die, so too in Christ shall all be brought to life, but each one in proper order: Christ the firstfruits; then, at his coming, those who belong to Christ; then comes the end, when he hands over the kingdom to his God and Father, when he has destroyed every sovereignty and every authority and power. For he must reign until he has put all his enemies under his feet. The last enemy to be destroyed is death. When everything is subjected to him, then the Son himself will also be subjected to the one who subjected everything to him, so that God may be all in all.